BRITISH INTERWAR AIRCRAFT

A PHOTOGRAPHIC GUIDE TO SURVIVING AIRCRAFT FROM 1918 TO 1939

LEE CHAPMAN

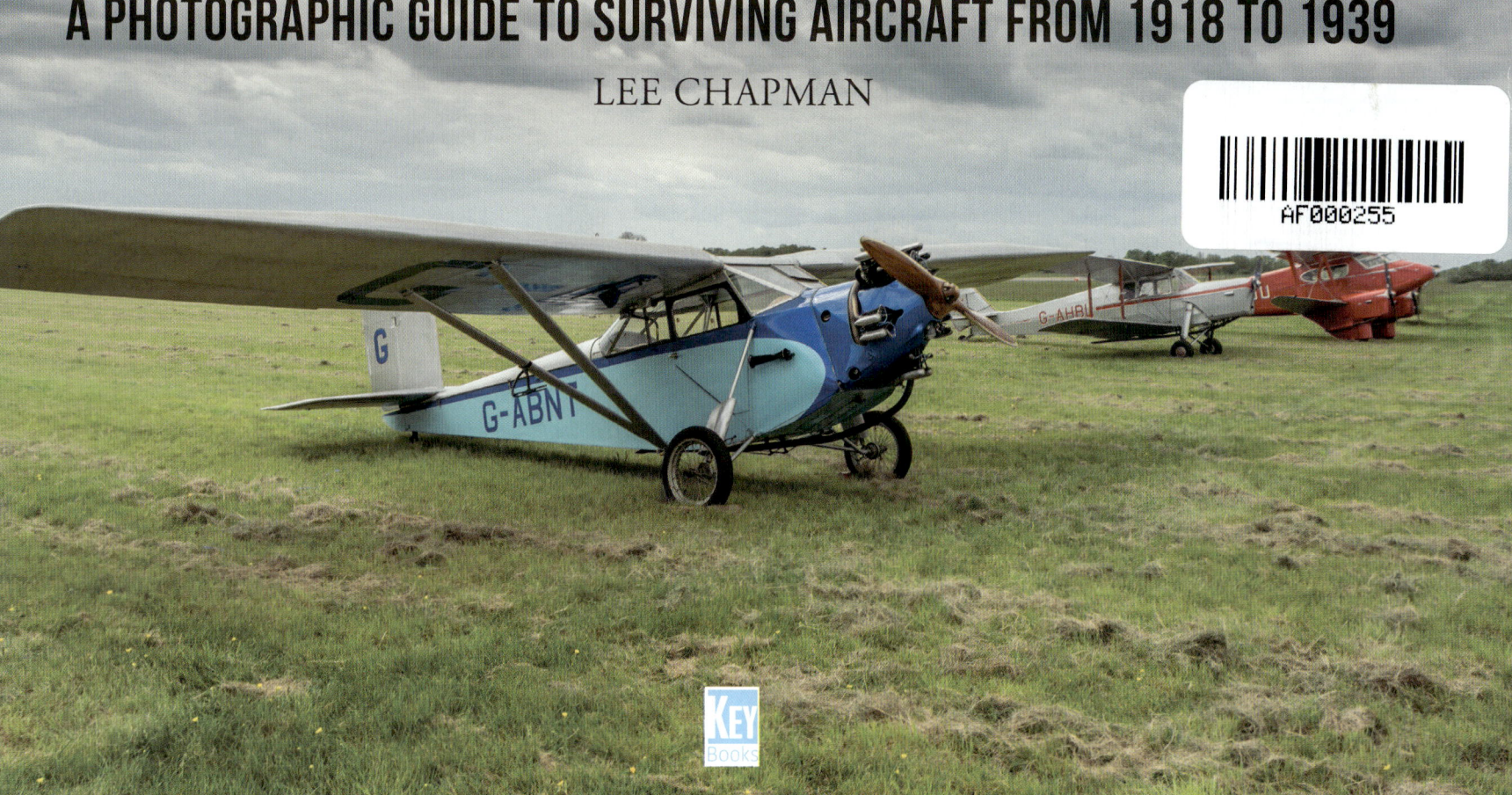

Front cover image: A 1930s two-seater turret fighter, the Hawker Demon.

Back cover image: Two original, airworthy 1930s racing aircraft: the Shuttleworth Collections DH88 Comet and Percival Mew Gull.

Title page image: A Civilian Coupé, de Havilland Dragonfly and de Havilland Hornet Moth, all operated by the Shipping and Airlines Collection based at Biggin Hill.

Contents page image: Two Percival Mew Gulls representing the golden age of air racing and record-breaking.

Author's Note

The author has tried to document as many of the surviving aircraft from between the two world wars that can be seen in the UK as possible. This was a time of transition for aviation, and many types of aircraft were designed and flown in this period for both civilian and military use. As this book concentrates on survivors, only a small fraction of the aircraft types in service between 1918 and 1940 are discussed. This book is not intended as a complete guide of all aircraft types of this vast period; this would run into many volumes. Instead, the book attempts to use the current survivors to tell the story of aviation during this period in general.

The aircraft from early on in this period were often fragile, lightweight and not built to last and, as such, few survive. Additionally, many of the more robust aircraft from the 1930s were either impressed into military service for World War Two or taken apart for spares and materials needed in the war effort. The following four years of war also took its toll on aircraft, in accidents and enemy bombing. Additionally, preserving aircraft was not common practice at the time and, as such, genuine complete survivors are rare. Therefore, many significant types used during the interwar period are now completely extinct and, therefore, these aircraft types are not fully discussed in this book.

Although some superb, significant aircraft were extent during the interwar years, unlike other periods in history, modern day rebuilds and replicas are less common. Some significant exceptions exist, and attempts have been made to capture this. Although this was a time for pioneering and record-breaking, the lack of noteworthy military campaigns during this period has meant that many incredible aircraft have been unable to avail themselves into public imagination. Additionally, some of the surviving aircraft types from this period only exist in private hands and are not on general display, making them challenging to access.

Published by Key Books
An imprint of Key Publishing Ltd
PO Box 100
Stamford
Lincs PE19 1XQ

www.keypublishing.com

The right of Lee Chapman to be identified as the author of this book has been asserted in accordance with the Copyright, Designs and Patents Act 1988 Sections 77 and 78.

Copyright © Lee Chapman, 2022

ISBN 978 1 80282 135 2

All rights reserved. Reproduction in whole or in part in any form whatsoever or by any means is strictly prohibited without the prior permission of the Publisher.

For more information about the author, please visit https://www.facebook.com/ChappersPhotography

Typeset by SJmagic DESIGN SERVICES, India.

CONTENTS

Preface	4
Chapter 1 – Introduction	6
Chapter 2 – After the Armistice: Post-World War One Military Aircraft	14
Chapter 3 – A Kickstart for British Light Aviation: Aircraft of the Lympne Trials	30
Chapter 4 – The British Aviation Industry Takes Off: Advanced Light Aircraft	44
Chapter 5 – The Beginning of Commercial Air Travel	62
Chapter 6 – The Golden Age: Racing and Record-breaking Aircraft	74
Chapter 7 – Silver Wings Part One: Military Biplanes of the 1930s	88
Chapter 8 – Silver Wings Part Two: The Hawker Air Force	98
Chapter 9 – Re-arming for War: Pre-World War Two Aircraft	110
Chapter 10 – Summary	124
Bibliography	128

PREFACE

Royal Aircraft Factory SE5a replica at Stow Maries Aerodrome just after sunrise.

Hawker Nimrod II K3661 G-BURZ representing the silver biplanes of the British military in the 1930s.

Aviation underwent a huge transformation between the two world wars. During World War One, the role of the aeroplane evolved from a stable, lumbering observation platform to a more agile fighter, capable of shooting down another aircraft. When the RAF was formed in 1918, Great Britain boasted the largest air force in the world. However, as soon as the armistice was declared, the nation prepared for peace and began a rapid disarmament. Many aircraft were surplus to requirements and either scrapped or sold for civilian use. This eventually led to the beginning of a civil aviation market. More people learned to fly, and a demand soon followed for purpose-built commercial, touring, racing and passenger aircraft.

When the British military was scaled back in 1919, the RAF was particularly hard hit and had to fight for its own survival. It was cut down to just 35,000 individuals, including 6,500 permanently commissioned officers. Meanwhile, civil aviation began to take off – a slow start initially, with surplus hastily adapted military aircraft, but eventually the commercial and recreational use of aircraft became widespread, and more innovated designs appeared. Pilots were focused on ever more daring feats and sought out records to break in speed, altitude, endurance and distance. This period is often referred to as the Golden Age of Aviation.

The period of peace was short-lived and, throughout the 1930s, the clouds of war began to loom once again. In response, Britain began to scale up its airpower, and a new wave of military aircraft designs began to emerge. During the first part of the decade, the RAF boasted an array of beautiful silver biplanes, which soon gave way to more sleek monoplane fighters and twin-engine medium-range bombers ready for the imminent war in Europe.

This book aims to capture the spirit of aviation during this period. It looks at many significant British aircraft types that were active between World War One and Two. Included are histories of both civil and military aircraft types that illustrate the history of how British aviation changed during the period. The story is told using high-quality images of surviving, replica and restored aircraft. It includes museum aircraft as well as a range of airworthy examples and restorations.

Acknowledgements

The author and publisher would like to thank the following organisations for permission to use copyright material in this book: Brooklands Museum, Cambridge Bomber and Fighter Society, Sleap Aircraft Recovery Museum, WW1 Aviation Heritage Trust, the Shuttleworth Collection, the Avro Heritage Museum, the Army Flying Museum, Biggin Hill Heritage Hangar, the Midland Air Museum, Solent Sky Museum, Stow Maries Great War Aerodrome, the Imperial War Museum and the RAF Museums for permission to photograph their exhibits on their sites. Every attempt has been made to seek permissions for copyright material and photographic rights in this book. However, if we have inadvertently used materials without permission, we apologise, and we will make the necessary correction at the first opportunity.

The author would also like to thank the team at Key Publishing; Georgia Massey for encouragement, motivation and support; Andy 'Loopy' Forester, Steve Nixon and Daniel Gooch for joining him on aircraft photography adventures. Finally, the author would also like to acknowledge the hard work of airshow organisers, warbird operators, restorers, homebuilders, conservators, reenactors and museum curators that keep the memories alive.

CHAPTER 1
INTRODUCTION

A collection of interwar aircraft designed by F G Miles: two Miles Magisters (on the flanks), a Southern Martlet (centre) and a Miles Hawk Speed Six (at the bottom).

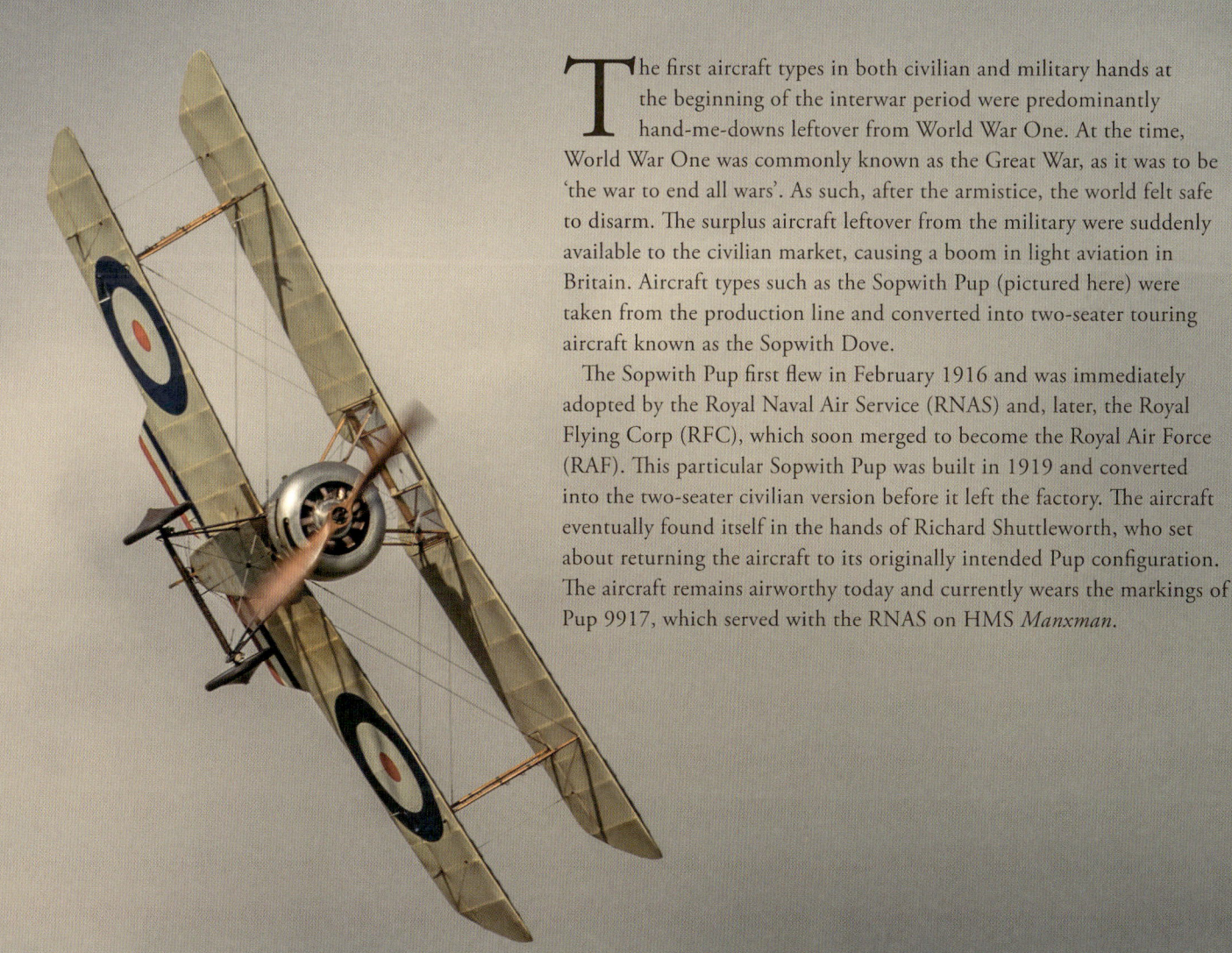

The first aircraft types in both civilian and military hands at the beginning of the interwar period were predominantly hand-me-downs leftover from World War One. At the time, World War One was commonly known as the Great War, as it was to be 'the war to end all wars'. As such, after the armistice, the world felt safe to disarm. The surplus aircraft leftover from the military were suddenly available to the civilian market, causing a boom in light aviation in Britain. Aircraft types such as the Sopwith Pup (pictured here) were taken from the production line and converted into two-seater touring aircraft known as the Sopwith Dove.

The Sopwith Pup first flew in February 1916 and was immediately adopted by the Royal Naval Air Service (RNAS) and, later, the Royal Flying Corp (RFC), which soon merged to become the Royal Air Force (RAF). This particular Sopwith Pup was built in 1919 and converted into the two-seater civilian version before it left the factory. The aircraft eventually found itself in the hands of Richard Shuttleworth, who set about returning the aircraft to its originally intended Pup configuration. The aircraft remains airworthy today and currently wears the markings of Pup 9917, which served with the RNAS on HMS *Manxman*.

A de Havilland DH60 Moth leads a Desoutter and Spartan Arrow over Old Warden Aerodrome.

The abundant supply of surplus military aircraft, coupled with post-war austerity, prevented any major developments in aircraft design in the years immediately after World War One. However, by the mid-1920s, light aviation began to find its feet. The de Havilland Aircraft Company was a leader in the market. Led by the brilliant Geoffrey de Havilland, they produced a huge range of light aircraft, predominantly targeting the civilian market, although success did follow in military tenders towards the end of the interwar years. Many other smaller aircraft companies appeared at this time, some of which were very short-lived.

In this image, the iconic and hugely successful de Havilland Moth (DH60X) leads the way, followed by a Desoutter I and a Spartan Arrow. Both the Desoutter and Spartan companies would only produce a small number of aircraft designs in their relatively brief periods of operation. The Desoutter aircraft company was founded in 1928 by Marcel Desoutter, who based his aircraft on a Dutch design. Sadly, the company folded in 1932 after producing just 41 aircraft. The Spartan Aircraft Company produced a similar number of aircraft over a five-year period before merging with Saunders-Roe in 1935.

A single Hawker Demon leads two Hawker Nimrod aircraft in a very rare Hawker biplane flypast.

Many of the larger aircraft companies that had achieved great success during World War One struggled to make ends meet with the sudden cancellation of military orders. Their woes were doubled when they were hit by crippling excess-profit tax bills from their wartime sales. As a result, many companies were forced to close or diversify away from the aviation industry. The Sopwith Aviation Company was one of the biggest casualties of this; having designed several outstanding aircraft for the war effort, it was a victim of its own success.

Fortunately, the brains behind many of these great aviation companies were determined to succeed and began to form new companies in the 1920s. Tommy Sopwith would team up with Harry Hawker, Fred Sigrist and Bill Eyre to form H G Hawker Engineering (later Hawker Aircraft); each contributed £5,000 towards the new venture. Sadly, Harry Hawker was killed in a flying accident in 1921, but the company that carried his name would produce an incredible array of military aircraft well into the 1960s. The company's dominance peaked in the 1930s, when Hawker aircraft were so common in the RAF that the force was mockingly referred to as the 'Hawker Air Force'.

go-to primary training aircraft throughout the majority of the 1930s. It was eventually replaced by another biplane, the de Havilland Tiger Moth, which would serve throughout World War Two and beyond. Whilst training units favoured biplanes for their docile characteristics, there were still several frontline biplanes in operation during World War Two.

Biplanes were very popular during World War One; the extra wing provided more lift, which aided the low-powered engines of the time. The struts and additional wing also gave the aircraft added stability. Many early monoplanes lacked the strength of biplanes and were vulnerable to g forces, which caused aircraft to break up in flight. Although technology improved this over time, the bias towards biplanes continued well into the 1920s and 1930s, for both the civilian and the military markets. As technology and confidence in designs progressed, the potential of the more aerodynamic monoplane became clear – once perfected there was no going back.

The RAF and Fleet Air Arm (FAA) still used biplanes in many roles into and throughout World War Two, even though the technology was long outdated. The Avro 621 Tutor (pictured in the foreground) was the RAF's

An Avro Tutor with its eventual replacement, the de Havilland Tiger Moth, in the background.

Introduction

Following World War One, aviation technology had made huge leaps forward, and for the first time in history, long-distance passenger flights became possible. At first, airships were popular in this role, but following the *Hindenburg* disaster, the flying boat became the first choice for long-haul passenger flights. Eventually, the limitations of operating aircraft from water led to the development of larger land-based passenger aircraft, which took over as the first choice for fee-paying passenger travel.

The British military also made good use of flying boats such as the Supermarine Stranraer (pictured here). They fulfilled maritime reconnaissance, search and rescue and anti-U-boat roles throughout the interwar period and into the early stages of World War Two. The Stranraer first flew in 1934 and was taken into RAF service three years later. Although it was withdrawn from frontline duties early in the war, it remained in service in the background until the end of the conflict, at which point 13 examples went into civilian services in Canada until 1958.

The period between the wars was characterised with daring and dramatic feats in aviation. It was the peak time for record-breaking, barn storming and air racing. Pioneers continued to develop better aircraft designs to fly faster, higher and further. During peacetime, aircraft designers were free to experiment and came up with new technologies that would prove invaluable when applied to military aircraft in World War Two.

The three iconic racing aircraft pictured here evoke the pioneering spirit of the interwar years. The DH88 Comet that leads the formation won the 1934 England to Australia Air Race and, after a brief period under evaluation in the RAF, set records for return flights to both New Zealand and the Cape in South Africa. The two other aircraft in this formation are Percival Mew Gulls, which dominated the late-1930s racing scene in the UK. Mew Gull G-AEXF (picture in the centre) is the exact aircraft that was flown by famous test pilot Alex Henshaw in February 1939 on a record-breaking trip to the Cape and back. His record of four days, ten hours and 16 minutes stood for over 70 years.

Supermarine Spitfire Mk I N3200 and Hawker Hurricane Mk I R4118.

The ultimate development in interwar aircraft design was the fast, streamlined, agile monoplane interceptor. Aircraft such as the Hawker Hurricane and Supermarine Spitfire first took to the air in the middle of the 1930s and boasted incredible performance well beyond the RAF's current biplane fighters. The Hawker Hurricane was the first 300mph fighter aircraft in RAF service, whilst the Spitfire, which arrived a year later, was faster still. Both the Spitfire and Hurricane were equipped with the powerful Rolls-Royce Merlin engine, retractable undercarriage and enclosed cockpits, together providing quantum leaps in performance over their biplane predecessors.

The Hawker Hurricane first entered RAF service in 1937, and by the time World War Two broke out, it was the dominate single-engine fighter in the service. Although the Spitfire soon followed the Hurricane into action, it equipped far fewer squadrons in 1939. Some biplanes still lingered on in frontline service in World War Two, but it was the monoplane that held the key to success in the Battle of Britain and beyond. The introduction of these iconic monoplane interceptors was a clear demonstration of how far aircraft technology had come during the interwar years. Sadly, their introduction also coincided with the end of peacetime, which brought a dramatic end to the Golden Age of Aviation.

CHAPTER 2
AFTER THE ARMISTICE:
POST-WORLD WAR ONE MILITARY AIRCRAFT

The Shuttleworth Collection's Sopwith Pup, which was originally built as a post-war civilian Sopwith Dove.

Although the RFC and RNAS had valiantly defended Britain during World War One, the increasingly devastating German attacks on London towards the end of 1917 prompted a review into British air power. Lt Gen Jan Smuts was commissioned to conduct the review and in his six-page report, known as the Smuts Report, he recommended the formation of an independent air force on par in status with the British Army and Royal Navy. Prime Minister David Lloyd George concurred, and the RAF was officially formed on 1 April 1918.

Britain was the first nation in the world to form its own standalone air force, which, on its formation, was equipped with 20,000 aircraft and over 300,000 men. This was the largest air force in the world at that time. A far cry from the four squadrons of ramshackle aircraft that plodded their way across the English Channel four years earlier. Although this was a new air force, the aircraft initially available were an eclectic mix of hand-me-downs from the RFC and RNAS. Even after the war, some of these outdated types lingered on in service for several years.

The Great War Society reenactors recreate a World War One aviation scene at Stow Maries with a collection of replica aircraft: Royal Aircraft Factory SE5a (flying), Sopwith Pup (foreground) and BE2c (background).

British Interwar Aircraft

The end of the war brought with it many cuts in defence spending and an overall reduction in the aircraft and personnel required for the RAF. The future of the RAF itself was in doubt and had to wait nine months to have its status confirmed. However, it would be cut down to just 35,000 individuals, including 6,500 permanently commissioned officers. Hugh Montague Trenchard is generally known as the 'father of the Royal Air Force'. He was already head of the RFC in the field and appointed as the first Chief of the Air Staff for the RAF in April 1918. After the war, Trenchard was able to guide the newly formed RAF through several political and financial challenges to create the foundations for the future, including setting up the RAF College at Cranwell, the world's first military air academy.

Despite the RAF being a new force, it initially relied on aircraft inherited from the RFC and RNAS, which included many aircraft that had long been outdated by technological advancements. Aircraft such as the Sopwith Pup (pictured below) had been in service since 1916 and two years of war had seen rapid developments in aviation. More recent types, such as the Sopwith Camel (pictured right), were more capable but not available in the numbers required, forcing obsolete aircraft to continue in frontline roles they were no longer suited for, even after the armistice.

The Shuttleworth Collection's reproduction Sopwith Camel, built to original specifications.

The first new aircraft type to enter service with the RAF was the Airco DH9a; even this was a modification of the DH9 (pictured here), which found its origins in the DH4, which had been in service for some time. Despite great advances in aeroplane technology, Britain was still playing catch-up with engine production. In the early stages of World War One, British aircraft were mostly powered by continental-built engines. As the war progressed, superb British engine designs had emerged from Bentley, Wolseley and Rolls-Royce. New aircraft designs like the DH9 were intended to take advantage of these new British engines. The first DH9s were fitted with Siddeley B H P (Beardmore-Halford-Pullinger) engines, which were eventually replaced with a more powerful, lightweight variation known as the Siddeley Puma. Both engines proved problematic in service, as they lacked the required power for carrying the heavy loads and were also plagued with reliability issues. Initially, the DH9 proved to be a less capable aircraft than the DH4 it was designed to replace. The arrival of the DH9a would rectify many of these issues.

Following the armistice, many DH9s were surplus to British requirements and therefore shipped abroad to other nations as part of the Imperial Gift scheme. Of the six remaining DH9s, only two are viewable in the UK, and this is only down to a chance find; leftover from the Imperial Gift, two airframes remained largely forgotten in Bikaner, India. Guy Black of Aero Vintage (Retrotec) managed to negotiate the return of these airframes to England and undertook a lengthy restoration in partnership with the Imperial War Museum (IWM). The result was the return of one to the air, whilst this one, D-5649, was prepared for static display at the IWM Duxford.

Despite its shortcomings, the Airco DH9 saw extensive service in the last few months of World War One. It was used in many bombing raids over the Western Front and also in anti-submarine patrols in the Middle East and the Indian sub-continent. After the war, it saw military service all over the world and was widely adopted for civilian use. Its last combat action with the RAF was in 1920 in Somalia, where it helped to bring a conclusion to the long-running Dervish War. The DH9 was used there for bombing campaigns against Mohammed Abdullah Hassan, the Mad Mullah.

The DH9 was the most produced aircraft of World War One. More than 4,000 were built, but very few have survived today. E8894 was built in the spring of 1918 by the Airco, based at Hendon. It is not thought to have played an active role in the war but was selected for transport to India following the armistice. From the two airframes recovered by Guy Black, it was selected as the most suitable for return to flight, and although a significant number of parts have been rebuilt, it maintains a high level of authenticity. It has recently returned to the skies and is now the only genuine World War One bomber flying anywhere in the world.

For its first new aircraft, the DH9a, the RAF would turn to America for a more reliable powerplant. It chose the 400hp Liberty 12 engine to power its new bomber. The team at Westland Aircraft were already experienced in building the DH9 and took the lead in the conversion to the new American engine. The result was a more powerful, reliable bomber that would equip No 110 Squadron of the RAF in France from 31 August 1918. After the war, the aircraft was so successful it would continue in service until 1931. Even then, the Westland Wapiti that was built to replace it used a vast amount of DH9a parts, making good use of the extensive stock of spares available. Geoffrey de Havilland's basic design layout was so effective that he used it for several light aircraft, including the iconic de Havilland Tiger Moth that would serve in the RAF for over 20 years.

The RAF Museum's DH9a (F1010) was built by Westland Aircraft Works at Yeovil in June 1918. It was one of the few to be built with an American 400HP Packard Liberty engine. It was delivered to No 110 Squadron at Kenley in Surrey, which was uniquely funded by His Serene Highness, the Nizam of Hyderabad, hence the markings on the side of the aircraft. F1010 was then flown to France, where it was often taken on bombing raids by its regular crew: pilot Captain Andrew Glover from Liverpool and observer Lt William George Lewis Badley from South Africa. The aircraft was abandoned in Germany after a minor landing accident. Here it was adopted by the German people, and, eventually, it was restored for display in the Berlin Air Museum only to be damaged by British bombs in World War Two. Following a brief stint in Poland after World War Two, F1010 was acquired by the RAF Museum and brought back to England in 1977.

The superlative Sopwith Snipe was among a new generation of aircraft to enter service at the end of World War One. The Snipe was the latest in a line of aircraft from the Sopwith 'zoo', tracing back its history from the Tabloid through to the Strutter, Pup and Camel. The Snipe was slightly smaller than the Camel, but the centre section of the upper wing was uncovered to give the pilot better visibility. It was also powered by a Bentley BR.2 rotary engine, giving it an impressive performance and a top speed of over 120mph. The new engine technology also supplied power for a heated cockpit and an oxygen supply for the pilot.

This Sopwith Snipe is a composite of various elements taken from other Snipes, including a significant number of parts from E6655. The aircraft was assembled by TVAL in New Zealand and arrived for display in the UK in 2012. E6655 was one of 150 Snipes ordered from Coventry Ordnance Works on 20 March 1918. It arrived with the RAF in 1919 and flew with No 1 Squadron from RAF Hinaidi in Iraq in 1926. The Bentley BR.2 engine is an original, and the tailplane was acquired from the Shuttleworth Collection, which had been using a Snipe tailplane on its Sopwith Pup. The rest of the parts were either newly rebuilt or salvaged from the RAF Museums' stores. It is now on display at the RAF Museum in Hendon.

The Sopwith Snipe was one of the most successful post-World War One fighters in the RAF. Less than 100 Snipes actually saw service during the war, as the hostilities were over before it could more widely equip the frontline squadrons. Many of the wartime orders of the Snipe were cancelled after the armistice, but production did continue into 1919, by which time almost 2,000 had been built. In 1919, a squadron of Sopwith Snipes were sent to Russia to intervene on behalf of the White Russians against the Bolsheviks during the Russian Civil War. One of these Snipes was captured by the Bolsheviks and pressed into service for them. The Sopwith Snipe also saw service in the Royal Canadian Air Force until 1923 and would remain on strength in the RAF until it was declared obsolete in 1928.

This replica Sopwith Snipe was built by TVAL (The Vintage Aviator Limited) in New Zealand. It is an exact reconstruction of Sopwith Snipe F2367 of No 70 Squadron, which was on occupational duties in Germany immediately after World War One. It is based in New Zealand but registered in the UK as G-CKBB. It was recently loaned to the WW1 Aviation Heritage Trust, making occasional appearances at UK airshows before returning to New Zealand in 2017.

The Royal Aircraft Factory SE5a was flown during World War One by most of the highest-scoring British aces, including Major Edward C 'Mick' Mannock, who scored 50 of his 75 kills in it. It had excellent speed and impressive range and was well-armed with its two .303 machine guns. It was highly manoeuvrable and, unlike the Sopwith Camel, was safe even for inexperienced pilots. Despite its success during World War One, its post-war career was brief and, by the end of 1919, the majority of SE5a's had been retired from the RAF. Many of these surplus aircraft were put up for sale on the civilian market, where they were adopted for many uses during the post-World War One years.

SE5a F904 is a typical example of this. It was purchased with several other SE5s (three of which still survive today) by Major J C Savage for his skywriting business. Savage made use of F904 for over ten years before putting the aircraft into long-term storage. It was eventually rediscovered and restored to its World War One configuration, including a refurbished 200hp Wolseley Viper engine. F904 is the only aircraft that achieved an air-to-air victory during World War One and is still airworthy. On 10 November 1918, Major C E M Pickthorn MC successfully destroyed a Fokker D.VII just over Chimay in Belgium. This was his last of five victories, giving him ace status on the final full day of war. The aircraft still wears the markings of No 84 Squadron as flown by Major Pickthorn when he achieved his last kill. It is now owned and operated by the Shuttleworth Trust.

During World War One, the use of flying boats, or 'seaplanes' as they were then known, grew rapidly. They were able to fly long missions over water and fulfil anti-shipping coastal patrols and search and rescue roles. Following the war, their size and capability increased further, making them some of the largest and widely used aircraft of the interwar period.

The Supermarine Southampton entered RAF service in 1925 to replace some of the ageing Felixstowe F-line of seaplanes which had been in service since World War One. The Southampton was designed by R J Mitchell based on his earlier civilian seaplane, the Swan. It proved to be one of the most successful flying boats ever, clocking up 11 years of service with the RAF. Its most notable interwar achievement was when four Southamptons undertook a long-distance demonstration tour of over 27,000 miles around the Far East in 1927 and 1928.

Supermarine Southampton Mk 1 N9899 (pictured here) joined RAF No 480 (Coastal Reconnaissance) Flight in 1925. It saw extensive service, undertaking many long-range patrols around the British Isles until it was wrecked on a breakwater at Portland during a strong gale in November 1928. Although the engines were salvaged and re-used, the hull was sold off and converted into a houseboat. It remained in situ for many years, but, by the late 1960s, the remains of N9899 were in a poor state and deemed an eyesore by the local council at Felixstowe where it was moored. The RAF Museum acquired it and began an extensive recovery and restoration plan, before eventually putting it on display at Hendon in 1995. It is the only surviving example anywhere in the world.

In 1919, the Vickers Aircraft Company, based at Brooklands, produced the Vickers Viking seaplane. It was the first amphibious aircraft produced by Vickers and was designed with military patrols in mind. However, the end of World War One meant that it was no longer required for this role. Instead, the Viking was used in Canada for surveying vast forests and in Switzerland for ferrying tourists. One was even produced for an unsuccessful attempt at flying all the way around the world. Several variants were produced, including the Mark VI, which was then considered so different it was given the new name Vulture.

This replica is based on the 1922 Mark IV Vickers 60 Viking and was built for the 1977 film *The People That Time Forgot*. It was left forgotten in Thorpe Park for several years before being transferred to the Booklands Museum, where the volunteers restored it to its former glory. It now represents G-EBED, which was the aircraft in which Australian brothers Keith and Ross Smith attempted to fly around the world in. Keith would later lose his life in another Vickers Viking, which crashed during a test flight from Brooklands in 1922. Fellow aviation pioneer John Alcock (see Chapter 6) would suffer a similar fate in this aircraft type too.

The Avro 504 was the first biplane produced by the now-famous Avro company. It was the most produced aircraft of World War One, and by the time production had ceased in 1932, over 10,000 had been built. Although it was quickly outdated as a frontline aircraft, its stable and reliable characteristics made it an ideal training aeroplane. It would remain as the main British military flight trainer until it was replaced in 1933 by the Avro Tutor. The Avro 504 went through many upgrades and modifications and was so successful that it remained operational at some level throughout most of the interwar period. Even after retirement, some Avro 504s were impressed back into military service when World War Two broke out. During the interwar period, over 300 504s were placed on the civil register and used for training, pleasure and occasional aerobatics.

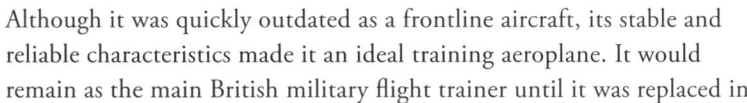

This original Avro 504k (G-ADEV) is owned and operated by the Shuttleworth Collection. G-ADEV was built in 1918 as a K variant but soon converted to a 504N, complete with radial engine. After seeing no action in World War One, G-ADEV entered civilian hands until 1939, when it was impressed back into military service for towing gliders and testing radar installations – a true testament to the longevity of the aircraft type. It has been restored to its original 504k layout and now wears the markings of a night fighter from No 77 Squadron, which was based at East Lothian in late 1918.

The 504 was one of the first aircraft that the then young designer Roy Chadwick would work on during his time with Avro. Chadwick would later go on to design some of the most iconic British aircraft of all time, including the Avro Lancaster. After the armistice, many war-surplus machines were adapted for civilian use and used by a variety of operators including C L Pashley Ltd, Cornwall Aviation Company, Eastbourne Aviation Company and the Grahame-White Aviation Company who all operated 12 aircraft each. It is thought that the many future British military pilots experienced their first flights in Avro 504s, as they were used for pleasure flights up and down the country during the 1920s. It is likely that this aircraft inspired many future Battle of Britain pilots to sign-up to the RAF.

The aircraft pictured here is a replica built in 1975 for the film *Aces High*. Although it cannot fly, it was built to be able to taxi. It was donated by the RAF Museum to the Brooklands Museum in 1987. Here the team of volunteers fitted an original Clerget engine and painted it to represent G-AACA, an aircraft that was operated by Brooklands School of Flying between 1928 and 1933. It provides an excellent representation of the aircraft used by the emerging flying clubs all over the UK during the interwar years.

Also known as the 'Brisfit', the Bristol F2 Fighter took its first flight in September 1916, and, after overcoming some early teething problems, it proved to be a quantum leap forward in performance over the BE2 that it was designed to replace. The Bristol Fighter was designed from the ground up as a fighter-reconnaissance aeroplane. Although it is a large aircraft compared to other contemporary fighters, its Rolls-Royce III V12 engine provides 275hp giving it an exceptional performance for the time. When it first entered service in 1917, it was operated cautiously by its pilots who were used to lumbering two-seaters; it was not until they learned to fly it more like a fighter that its fearsome reputation was earned. After the war, the F2b remained in RAF service until 1932, where it was primarily used as an Army Co-operation aircraft in Iraq and India. It too was converted for civilian use as the Bristol Type 47 Tourer, which benefited from a closed canopy and cockpit.

Eight original Bristol F2s have survived, three of these remain airworthy, including one based in the UK with the others in Canada and New Zealand. This example, E2581 (pictured left), is the most authentic surviving Bristol Fighter. It was displayed at the IWM's Lambeth site for many years, before being moved to Duxford in the 1980s. E2581 was built by the British Colonial Aeroplane (Bristol) Company in September 1918. It was issued to No 39 Home Defence Squadron at North Weald in Essex right at the end of the war. It served for the newly formed RAF until it was transferred to the museum in 1923.

Bristol F2b D8096 served with No 208 Squadron in Turkey in 1923. In 1952, after a long period in storage, the Bristol Aeroplane Company restored the aircraft to flight; it has been flying with the Shuttleworth Trust ever since. The Bristol F2b proved to be one of the most successful aircraft of the war and continued in military service for many years afterwards. It is pictured here wearing its original No 208 Squadron markings (see below left), as it was seen until 2020. It is also pictured in its current scheme (see below right), B1162/F of No 22 squadron, which was flown by Sgt Ernest John Elton who was the highest-scoring British non-commissioned officer pilot of the RFC during World War One.

The immediate post-World War One years saw a gradual decline in British aircraft output; very few new designs emerged, and the aircraft produced for war were forced to infill several peacetime roles. Whilst this was bad for the industry, the sheer number of aircraft available made it easy for the would-be pilot to gain their first experiences of flight.

CHAPTER 3
A KICKSTART FOR BRITISH LIGHT AVIATION: AIRCRAFT OF THE LYMPNE TRIALS

The Shuttleworth Collection's DH60 Moth.

The rapid disarmament at the end of World War One led to the cancellation of many orders for wartime aircraft. The major aircraft companies that had proved successful during the war were left facing financial ruin unless they could evolve and adapt. Some moved out of aviation altogether, whilst others began re-designing aircraft for civilian use. The Sopwith company, who had led the way with military aircraft designs during the war, produced the civilian Dove in 1919. This was a two-seater version of the wartime Sopwith Pup. When military orders were cancelled, some Pups were taken off the production line and converted to Doves. It was marketed as a sporting and utility aeroplane and, like its predecessor, performed well in its roll. However, the market was flooded with cheap surplus military aircraft and, during a period of austerity, few could afford the luxuries of owning an aeroplane.

Only ten Doves were produced, one of which was a single-seater. The only survivor has now been re-configured into a Sopwith Pup. The Sopwith Dove pictured here is a replica currently based at Old Warden in Bedfordshire. It was built by Skysport Engineering in 1993 using an original 1919 80hp Le Rhône engine and some original parts from the Shuttleworth Collection's Pup, which was originally constructed as a Dove. It is registered as G-EAGA and wears the markings of Dove 3004/1, which was registered to the Sopwith Aviation & Engineering Company on 3 July 1919.

The vast supply of military surplus aircraft immediately after the war was one of the biggest challenges to aircraft manufacturers. It was hard to design a new product that could be sold at a competitive price in comparison to what was on offer from the Aircraft Disposal Company. Frederick Handley Page had acquired the entire stock of around 100,000 British military surplus aircraft, complete with spares from the Government Disposals Board for a fee of £1,080,000. Its estimated value was around £100 million. He formed the Aircraft Disposal Company in 1920 to broker sales of these aircraft to the public. Handley Page was soon able to amass over £500,000 in profits, with enough stock leftover for another ten years. The unfortunate impact of this success was the lack of new aircraft designs and the forced closures of many great British aviation companies.

One of the benefactors of this new scheme was Alan Cobham who, through his Berkshire Aviation Company, purchased a single Avro 504k from the Aircraft Disposal Company. Cobham took the three-seater on a tour of the UK in 1919, offering joyrides to paying passengers. From these humble beginnings, Cobham would perhaps do more than any other pioneer for British civil aviation. By 1932, he was taking his 'aviation days' to no less than 110 locations a year, performing air displays and offering passenger flights to thousands of customers.

This Avro 504k is the amalgamation of two original airframes. The fuselage was taken from Avro 504K G-EBJE, and the wings are from Avro 548A G-EBKN. The Avro 548A was an aircraft developed later by Avro but heavily based on the 504. This aircraft is on static display at the RAF Museum in Hendon.

The lack of new British aircraft designs did not go unnoticed, and a few pioneering individuals set about reversing this. In 1923, George Granville Sutherland-Leveson-Gower, the 5th Duke of Sutherland and the Under-Secretary of State for Air, put up a £500 prize for the British designer who could produce the most economical aircraft. This was essentially determined by how far an aircraft could fly on one gallon of fuel. The *Daily Mail* also offered a £1,000 prize for any aircraft that could fly 50 miles over a triangular course, powered by an engine of less than 750cc capacity. These trials first took place in 1923 at Lympne in Kent and therefore became known as the Lympne Light Aircraft Trials. Further trials also took place in 1924 and 1926 at the same location. Several aircraft manufacturers entered designs, including household names such as Avro, Hawker (then known as H G Hawker Engineering Company), de Havilland and Vickers.

In 1923, the two prizes were merged and then split between two winners, the Air Navigation and Engineering Company (ANEC) Monoplane and English Electric Wren (pictured here), both of which recorded 87.5 miles per gallon. The Wren was designed by W O Manning for the English Electric Company based in Preston, Lancashire. It was built using a wooden airframe covered with fabric and powered by a 298cc ABC motorcycle engine. Despite its success in the trials, orders were not forthcoming and only three were ever built, one of which survives and remains airworthy today. This Wren was originally built as a Competition No 4 aeroplane for the trials but was later re-built using some components from the other Wrens, courtesy of the Science Museum. It is currently operated by the Shuttleworth Collection and performs occasional flights at Old Warden when the weather conditions allow.

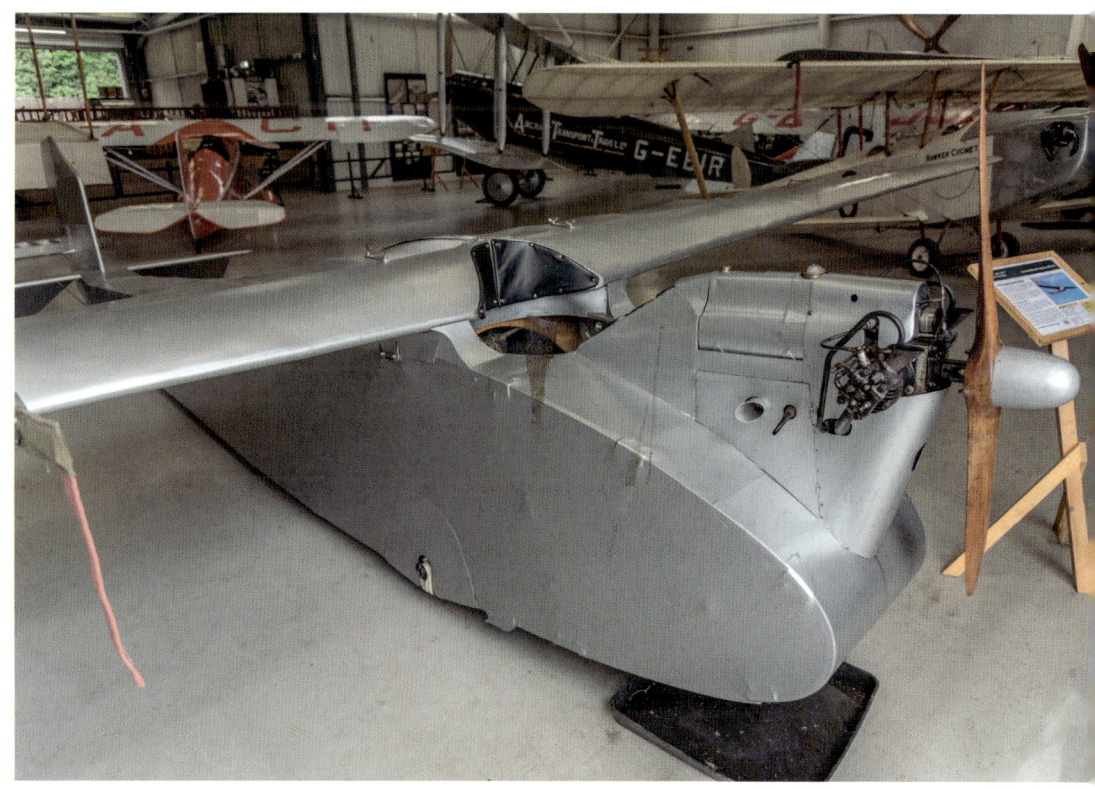

To find a more practical aircraft, the rules for the 1924 Lympne trials changed. They sought to find a two-seater light aircraft with full dual controls and a maximum engine size of 1,100cc. Once again, the trials attracted aviation's top names including Bristol, Supermarine, Avro and Hawker. The conditions of the competition proved a real challenge for the technology of the day, and only the Beardmore Wee Bee and Bristol Brownie were able to complete the speed trials successfully. The Wee Bee was the fastest and took the first prize.

Encouraged by its success in 1923, ANEC designed an improved two-seater version of its ANEC I, which was given the designation ANEC II. The ANEC II was designed by William Shackleton and powered by a 1,100cc V twin Anzani engine. Although the aircraft looked promising, the engine proved unreliable, and the aircraft missed the 1924 trails because of a malfunctioning carburettor. The ANEC II eventually passed into civilian hands and was fitted with a more robust Bristol Cherub engine, which enabled the aircraft to join the late 1920s air racing circuit. It is still airworthy and now owned and operated by the Shuttleworth Collection and has been reconfigured to its original specification.

In the 1924 Lympne trials, there was also a prize for the shortest take-off and landing runs. The Bristol Brownie also took first place in this award, with the Hawker Cygnet coming in second place with a landing run of just 66.7 yards. The Hawker Cygnet was designed by Sydney Camm, who would later be responsible for some of Hawker's most famous aircraft, including the Hurricane and Hunter. The Cygnet was built using a wooden airframe covered in fabric, with a dual-control tandem cockpit layout. The original prototype was powered by a 34hp Anzani engine, but the second and only other Cygnet was given an ABC Scorpion III engine, both of which gave similar levels of performance.

With no trails taking place at Lympne in 1925, the rules were once again tweaked for the 1926 event. The organisers were still looking for a practical two-seater, this time with a maximum weight limit rather than an engine power limit. The prize money was also increased to £5,000 in total, put up alone by the *Daily Mail*, as the interest from the Air Ministry had now disappeared. This time the prize would be awarded to the all-round winner capable of carrying a fixed load over a total distance over 1,994 miles. The rules also stipulated an all-British design and, unsurprisingly, the prize money attracted several entrants from some famous manufacturers. The prize money was split over the top three places, with the top two spots both going to Hawker Cygnets. The first was flown by Paul Bulman on behalf of the Hawker factory. Second prize was won by the Royal Aircraft Establishment's (RAE) Aero Club and flown by J S Chick. Both aircraft were powered by a Bristol Cherub engine, which proved much more reliable than the engines used in the 1924 competition.

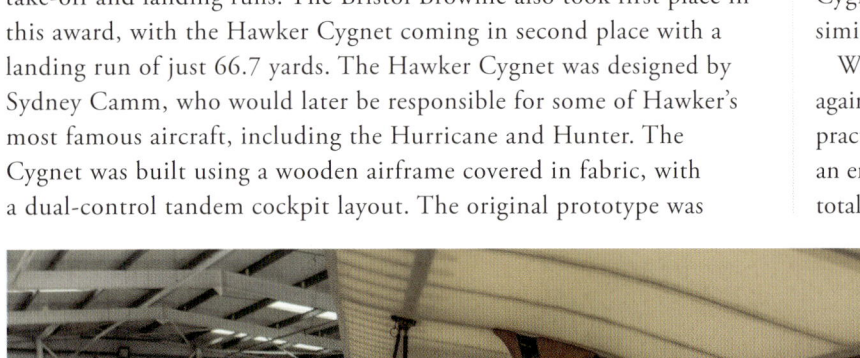

The Cygnet (pictured left) is an airworthy replica registered as G-CAMM in honour of its famous designer. It wears the markings of the original aircraft (G-EBJH) that achieved third place and a prize of £100 for take-off and landing in 1924.

This example was built by Don Cashmore in 1993 and, although it is powered by a more modern Mosler flat twin engine, it is otherwise authentic to the original design. It is now based at Old Warden and operated there as part of the Shuttleworth Collection.

The 1926 winning Hawker Cygnet (G-EBMB) (pictured right and below) has survived and is on display at the RAF Museum in Cosford, Shropshire. This example would go on to take the overall prize in the 1926 trials, as discussed on the next page. It remained airworthy until 1929 and even entered the Bournemouth Easter air races in 1927. After a long period in storage, it was restored to flight in May 1950 when it enjoyed a decade of flying in various events including the 50 Years of Flight celebration at Hendon in 1951. It has been on static display since 1972 at the RAF Museum.

Another company entering the Lympne trials was the Parnall Aircraft Company, originally known as George Parnall and Company. The company had evolved from a wood-working company into a significant aircraft designer and producer during World War One. Following the war, it turned its hand to civilian aircraft and put forward the Parnall Pixie aircraft to compete in the trials. Although this predominately competed as a monoplane, the designers produced an adaptable aircraft that could also be flown as a biplane. In 1924, the Parnall Pixie II was flown by Capt Norman Macmillan, who won the Abdulla speed prize after achieving a speed of over 76mph. The updated Parnall Pixie III dropped out mid-way through the 1924 trials but achieved a respectable fourth place in 1926.

The remains of one of the three Parnall Pixies built is currently in deep storage at the Midland Air Museum in Coventry. The only other aircraft left from the Parnall company's interwar legacy is this Parnall Elf, which is currently based at Old Warden with the Shuttleworth Collection. The Elf was a two-seater light touring aircraft, designed to compete with the de Havilland Moth. Three of these were built at its factory in Yate between 1928 and 1932. However, it was not a success, and after a damming report from the testing at Martlesham Heath in 1934, no further aircraft were built.

The de Havilland company also entered the Lympne trials, producing its first light aircraft for the 1923 competition. It opted for a lightweight, small, low-winged single-seat monoplane, the DH53, known as the Hummingbird. Although neither of the two Hummingbirds in the trials won a prize, there were signs that this was a promising design when Major Hemming flew his DH53 59.3 miles on one gallon of fuel. After the 1923 Lympne trials, Geoffrey de Havilland decided to break away from the Lympne trials limitations to produce a scaled-down version of his DH51. He wanted a small but comfortable two-seater aircraft capable of taking hard knocks and flying across the country with a reliable engine. The first line of DH60 aircraft were powered by an engine designed by Major Frank Halford, known as the Cirrus I. The aircraft was therefore designated the DH60 Cirrus Moth.

In 1925, the Air Ministry sponsored the opening of five geographically spread flying clubs in Newcastle, the Midlands, Yorkshire, Lancashire and London. The clubs were supported by the Air Ministry to help boost civil aviation and, therefore, re-start the floundering aviation industry. Some of the first aircraft taken on as part of this sponsorship scheme were DH60 Moths, including G-EBLV (pictured here). This DH60 Cirrus Moth (G-EBLV) is now owned and operated by BAE Systems as part of its heritage flight. It was built in 1925 and is the oldest surviving DH60.

The first flight of a DH60 Cirrus Moth took place on 22 February 1925, flown by Geoffrey de Havilland himself. It was the beginning of a large family of aircraft known collectively as Moths. Over 2,000 DH60 Moths were built between 1925 and 1934. Their design evolved and included eight different engines, each providing more power than the last. The Moth had a conventional fabric cover over a wooden airframe and proved to be both efficient and economical to run. It was the chosen mount of many pioneering aviators, including Amy Johnson and Alan Cobham.

Recognising the limitations of the Lympne trials, the de Havilland company did not produce an aircraft for the 1924 competition, but it did enter the DH60 Cirrus Moth into the 1926 trials. Although it failed to achieve a placing, hindsight has proven it to be the biggest success of the Lympne trials. The aircraft type would go on to achieve considerable commercial success, and, today, around 40 DH60s are thought to remain intact. The aircraft pictured here is a DH60x Moth that was built in 1928. It was initially used at the Brooklands School of Flying, where it was powered by a Cirrus I engine. In 1932, Richard Shuttleworth learned to fly in this aircraft and later purchased it, bringing it home to Old Warden Aerodrome, where it has remained ever since. It now holds the record for an aircraft being continually based at the same airfield for the longest period of time.

The folding wings of the DH60 Moth made it ideal to store in a small space, perfect for the small airfield.

The final development of the DH60 Moth series was the Moth Major, which was powered by a 130hp Gipsy Major engine; this gave it a maximum speed of 113mph and enabled it to climb at a rate of around 900ft per minute, double the rate of the first Cirrus Moth. The Gipsy Major engine was essentially a slightly improved Gipsy II, which had been inverted to allow for a cleaner, lower engine installation within the aircraft. This engine itself proved so successful that it would go on to power many iconic aircraft including the de Havilland Tiger Moth and de Havilland Canada (DHC) Chipmunk.

The aircraft pictured here (G-ACGZ) is a DH60GIII Moth Major, which often flies as part of the Tiger Nine aircraft display team. The team regularly flies nine DH Moth type aircraft (mostly Tiger Moths) at airshows in the UK. It shows how far light aircraft design had come since the beginning of the Lympne trials. Aircraft were now more reliable and much more capable. Without the incentives laid down in the Lympne trials, it may have taken considerably longer for the British light aviation industry to find its wings.

DH60GIII Moth Major G-ACGZ leads two DH82 Tiger Moths during part of the Tiger Nines display at the Midlands Air Festival.

CHAPTER 4
THE BRITISH AVIATION INDUSTRY TAKES OFF: ADVANCED LIGHT AIRCRAFT

A de Havilland Leopard Moth displaying at Old Warden.

The British Aviation Industry Takes Off: Advanced Light Aircraft

Following the initial lull in new aircraft designs and production after World War One, the British light aircraft industry began to find its wings in the mid-1920s. The Lympne trials had encouraged experimentation and more individuals were learning to fly at the emerging aero clubs across the UK. Without government support and military orders, most light aircraft designs developed during this time were short-lived and only produced in low numbers. Many small aircraft companies emerged during this period. Some, such as de Havilland, would go on to achieve considerable success, whilst others such as the Civilian Aircraft Company would simply fade away after producing only one aeroplane.

The Civilian Aircraft Company was formed in 1928 by Harold Boultbee who had recently left Handley Page. It produced just one aircraft design, of which only five were ever built. Remarkably, one of these has survived and is still airworthy. The aircraft was the Civilian Coupé, which was a high-winged monoplane and the first two-seater monoplane built in the UK with an enclosed cockpit. Despite being quite advanced for the time, sales were not forthcoming, and the company went bankrupt in 1933. G-ABNT is owned and operated by Shipping and Airlines, based at Biggin Hill. It was built in Hedon, near Hull, and was the third of five aircraft produced. It was nicknamed 'Bunty' and issued the registration number 3271 on 23 June 1931. G-ABNT was flown for six years before being put into storage and forgotten about for 38 years. It was eventually purchased and restored by Philip Mann, who then owned Shipping and Airlines. G-ABNT still flies today and is an occasional visitor to airshows and events in the UK.

In 1926, Frederick George Miles established the Southern Aircraft Company at Shoreham in Sussex. Miles acquired an Avro Baby aircraft. He completely rebuilt its wooden airframe and installed a 75hp ABC engine. The resulting aeroplane was found to have excellent flying characteristics when Miles test flew the aircraft himself. The aircraft eventually became known as the Martlet, named after the Sussex heraldic emblem. After the initial prototypes were built, a further five production machines were produced, each with slightly different specifications and engines. Although some of the aircraft entered the King's Cup Air Race, they were not a success. However, they did prove themselves as aerobatic machines and laid down the foundations for F G Miles' outstanding career in aircraft design.

This Martlet, G-AAYX, was owned for several years by Miles himself. It was his personal aircraft whilst he was based in Woodley near Reading. During World War Two, G-AAYX was put into storage before being resurrected by the Butlins holiday camp in Pwllheli, Wales, for holidaymakers' pleasure flights. Following this brief stint at Butlins, it was put into storage for over 30 years. It eventually passed into the hands of the Shuttleworth Trust, where it received some much-needed restorative work before being returned to the air in 2000. It is still a regular flyer at Shuttleworth airshows today.

Following the success of the Southern Martlet, F G Miles joined up with Charles Powis and Jack Phillips in a new venture in the early 1930s, known initially as Phillips & Powis Aircraft. The company was based on Woodley Aerodrome near Reading. F G Miles was the chief designer and, as such, the aircraft produced were often given his name. In 1936, Rolls-Royce invested in the firm and the company would go on to produce several successful military training aircraft such as the Miles Magister and Master. Although the aircraft were produced under the 'Miles' name, the company was not formally given the title Miles Aircraft Limited until 1943.

The Miles M3 Falcon (pictured here) was one of the earlier designs produced by Phillips & Powis Aircraft. It was based on the already successful Miles Hawk Trainer aircraft but was adapted for better passenger comfort and re-designed as a touring aircraft. The prototype was given extra fuel tanks and flown in the MacRobertson England to Australia Air Race. Success was not forthcoming. It took over 27 days to reach Australia and, as such, did not impact on the race itself. The return journey was different: the Falcon broke the record and got home in just under 8 days. Following this feat, orders were place for 29 Miles Falcons in the first year, and six variants were eventually spurned. This aircraft, G-AEEG, was built in 1936 and saw service during World War Two with the Swedish Air Force. In 1979, G-AEEG won the King's Cup Air Race at 43 years old. It is currently owned and operated by Shipping and Airlines.

The Air Ministry also saw the potential of Miles' aircraft designs, and, in 1937, it requested its own version of the civilian Hawk Trainer to close the gap in fighter pilot training between the Tiger Moth biplane and the new monoplane fighters. The new derivative became known as the Miles Magister (pictured right). It retained the fixed undercarriage and

open cockpit and was also powered by a Gipsy Major, but also shared some characteristics with the Spitfire and Hurricane. It was generally considered a successful second-phase trainer by the RAF, and many of the airframes were adopted for air racing after World War Two. Just before the war, the Air Ministry also took on the Miles Master as an advanced monoplane trainer to close the gap in the training syllabus.

This Magister (pictured left) was registered as V1075 in the RAF, where it served until 1942. V1075 has passed through several owners, and it was restored to flight in 1990 and is now owned by one of the Shuttleworth Collection's pilots, David Bramwell. It is based at Old Warden Aerodrome. No complete Miles Masters have survived, but this Kestrel engine from a Master wreck has been recovered and displayed by the Wartime Aircraft Recovery Group at Sleap Airfield in Shropshire.

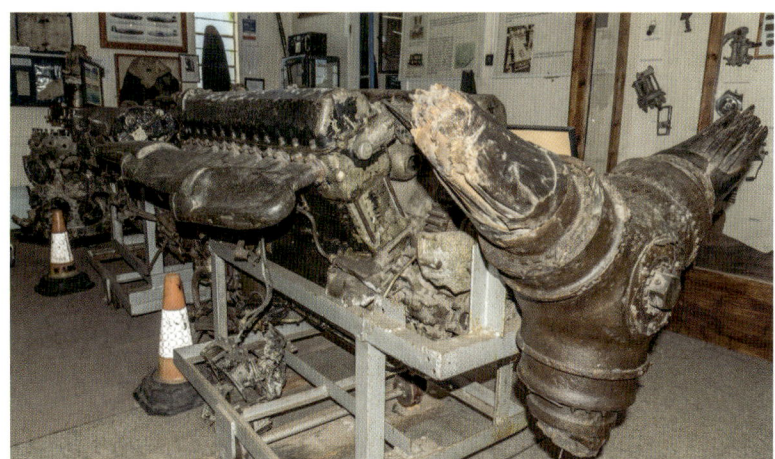

In 1928, Oliver Simmons started an aircraft company known as Simmonds Aircraft. Its first aircraft, the Simmonds Spartan, was produced in a factory in Woolston, Hampshire, and proved popular, with 50 examples being produced. Unfortunately, the company suffered financial difficulties and took on investments from Whitehall Securities, changing the name of the company to Spartan Aircraft Limited. The first new design under this guise was the Spartan Arrow, a two-seater biplane. Fifteen examples of the Arrow were built, including two prototypes. The aircraft were mostly powered by de Havilland Gipsy II engines, but other engine types were also tested on the design.

In 1931, Whitehall Securities also invested heavily in Saunders-Roe, and despite some promising aircraft produced by the Spartan factory, the company was soon merged into Saunders-Roe and ceased to build aircraft from 1935. G-ABWP is the sole surviving Spartan Arrow, powered by a Cirrus Hermes II; it is still airworthy today. The aircraft was first owned by Richard Shuttleworth, whose name is now synonymous with vintage aircraft through the work of the Shuttleworth Trust at Old Warden. G-ABWP is currently owned by Richard Blain and based at Redhill Aerodrome in England. It is seen here appearing at one of the Shuttleworth airshows.

A Spartan Arrow passing over a Desoutter.

The de Havilland DH82 Tiger Moth is probably the most famous interwar light aircraft design. It was based around Geoffrey de Havilland's DH60T Moth. Incredibly, no drawing was ever made during the design process. Instead, designers Arthur Hagg and Frank Trounson were given the DH60T aircraft which they took apart and reconfigured several times. Through a process of trial and error, the pair came up with the hugely successful biplane that would go on to be the mainstay of RAF primary training from the mid-1930s until well into the 1950s.

The new Tiger Moth had been given an inverted Gipsy III or Gipsy Major engine, which greatly improved the forward view, ideal for the excited trembling recruit as he taxied out for the first time. As well as extensive military service, the Tiger Moth was also built for civilian use. Although when war broke out, many civilian-registered aircraft were impressed into service. The adaptable Tiger Moth was also used as a maritime reconnaissance aircraft, and, during the darkest days of World War Two, some were even kitted out as light bombers to attack any potential landing forces if they reached British soil. Fortunately, this was never the case.

Today, the Tiger Moth remains a popular civilian aeroplane and over 250 are thought to be airworthy throughout the world. There are also numerous examples on static display in museums. The de Havilland 82 Tiger Moth II G-AOJK was built in 1939 and served with the RAF as R4896. It remained with the RAF until the mid-1950s when it passed into civilian ownership. It is currently owned by Peter Green and is seen here at Sleap Airfield in Shropshire.

The British Aviation Industry Takes Off: Advanced Light Aircraft

The prototype de Havilland DH82 Tiger Moth made its maiden flight on 26 October 1931. It was the first aircraft in the Moth series to feature swept-back and staggered wings, which were designed partially to enable quicker exit from the aircraft during an emergency. The first 35 Tiger Moths joined the RAF Central Flying School in 1932; more orders soon followed. In 1934, an improved version, known in the RAF as the Tiger Moth II, was produced featuring a more powerful Gipsy Major engine and plywood decking in the rear fuselage replacing the fabric. Further modifications included anti-spinning strakes on the sides of the rear fuselage (see insert).

The Tiger Moth pictured here, T6818, was built by Morris Motors in 1944 and now flies regularly for the Shuttleworth Trust based in Old Warden. It currently wears the markings of the RAF Central Flying School Aerobatics Team.

The de Havilland Tiger Moth's docile flying characteristics made it ideal for thousands of future frontline pilots to get their first taste of flying. As the likelihood of war increased during the 1930s, more and more Tiger Moths were ordered. The priority in production went to the Air Ministry, but 25 foreign air forces also used the Tiger Moth as their trainer. Tiger Moths equipped both the Elementary and Reserve Flying Schools in the UK, as well as many private aero clubs at the time too.

When World War Two broke out, the paint scheme on the Tiger Moth was changed from the all-over yellow to a more conservative look, with camouflage on the top of the aircraft to help disguise it on the ground. The differences between the two schemes can be seen in the images below of two aircraft from the Tiger Nines Display Team. Although never required, 1,500 sets of specially designed bomb racks were also sent out to elementary flying training schools for use in case of invasion. Towards the end of the war, some Tiger Moths were even equipped to carry out the medical evacuation role via removing the rear cockpit and replacing it with the space for a stretcher.

The success of the de Havilland Tiger Moth design led to several variants and spin-offs. One notable version was the DH82B Queen Bee. This was a pilotless, radio-controlled version of the popular trainer. The aircraft was referred to as a 'drone', referring to the male bee, which makes one flight in search of its queen, thus making this aircraft the first drone in the RAF. The Queen Bee was used to help train the anti-aircraft gunners from 1935 onwards, whose role in the protection of Great Britain during World War Two cannot be underestimated. Instead of the fabric-covered metal frame, the Queen Bee was produced using a spruce and plywood frame, as this was cheaper and buoyant in the event of a ditching. The aircraft could still be flown by a pilot from the front cockpit, but the rear was fitted with a pneumatic radio-controlled device to be operated from the ground.

Around 400 Queen Bees were built, and, despite their wooden structure and somewhat hazardous occupation, there are still two surviving in the UK today. One can be found at the de Havilland Aircraft Museum in London (see right) and the other (see below), LF858, is still airworthy and based at RAF Henlow in Bedfordshire. LF858 has now been fitted with full flying controls in the rear cockpit and often performs balloon popping and aerial stunts as part of Captain Neville's Flying Circus.

The de Havilland company continued to dominate the light aircraft market for the duration of the 1930s and designed several ever-improving aircraft that became faster, more reliable and, most importantly, more comfortable. The DH85 Leopard Moth was a three-seater monoplane with an enclosed cabin designed for the luxury touring market. It first flew in 1933 and, like many de Havilland designs, was entered into the King's Cup Air Race that year to demonstrate its capabilities. Geoffrey de Havilland piloted the aircraft to victory with an average speed of just under 140mph. Unsurprisingly, many orders were forthcoming, and over 130 Leopard Moths were built.

Leopard Moths proved popular as air taxis, and several were put to work for companies such as Olley Air Service, Air Commerce and Air Taxis. The type was also chosen for record attempts and long-distance flights. The first such flight in a Leopard Moth was undertaken by Neville Stack and F E Clifford, who flew all the way to Senegal in 1934, recording their experiences on a Dictaphone. A few weeks later, Bernard Rubin and Ken Waller used a Leopard Moth to survey the route to Australia in preparation for the MacRoberston Air Race. They broke the record on the return journey after arriving home eight days and 12 hours after they left.

Today, there are six airworthy Leopard Moths on the UK civil register, including G-ACMA (pictured left), which was built in 1934. It has recently been restored to its original pre-war configuration, including its National Benzole petroleum company paint scheme. G-ACMA was impressed into military service during World War Two and given the serial number BD148. G-ACMN (pictured below) was built in 1934 and was used for charter flying with Personal Airways based in Croydon from 1936. It too was impressed into military service in 1939. During the war, G-ACMN was given the designation X9381 and served as a communication aircraft before being sold back to de Havilland Aircraft in 1946.

The de Havilland company continued to explore ways to enhance the light aircraft flying experience. One such experiment was the DH87 Hornet Moth. The Hornet Moth featured a side-by-side cabin layout. Prior to this, most passengers sat behind the pilot, as it was felt they may be a distraction. This new layout not only appealed to the luxury civilian aeroplane owner but was also a revelation for ab initio flight training. The Hornet Moth was fitted with the same type of rear fuselage as the Leopard Moth, but the front section was a completely new design, built of welded steel tubing. The prototype was taken for its maiden flight by Geoffrey de Havilland on 9 May 1934 and was of course entered for the King's Cup race shortly afterwards. Despite achieving an average speed of 127mph, the Hornet Moth was eliminated in the heats of the 1934 race.

The Hornet Moth is also noteworthy for being one of the first aircraft to be exhaustivity tested prior to being offered for sale. Although standard practice today, it was not common for so many tests to be undertaken on aircraft. After issues with two previous designs, the DH86 Express Air Liner and the DH87 Puss Moth, de Havilland was keen to get the Hornet Moth right before it was released. The first production aircraft

The British Aviation Industry Takes Off: Advanced Light Aircraft

Today, there are six airworthy Leopard Moths on the UK civil register, including G-ACMA (pictured left), which was built in 1934. It has recently been restored to its original pre-war configuration, including its National Benzole petroleum company paint scheme. G-ACMA was impressed into military service during World War Two and given the serial number BD148. G-ACMN (pictured below) was built in 1934 and was used for charter flying with Personal Airways based in Croydon from 1936. It too was impressed into military service in 1939. During the war, G-ACMN was given the designation X9381 and served as a communication aircraft before being sold back to de Havilland Aircraft in 1946.

The de Havilland company continued to explore ways to enhance the light aircraft flying experience. One such experiment was the DH87 Hornet Moth. The Hornet Moth featured a side-by-side cabin layout. Prior to this, most passengers sat behind the pilot, as it was felt they may be a distraction. This new layout not only appealed to the luxury civilian aeroplane owner but was also a revelation for ab initio flight training. The Hornet Moth was fitted with the same type of rear fuselage as the Leopard Moth, but the front section was a completely new design, built of welded steel tubing. The prototype was taken for its maiden flight by Geoffrey de Havilland on 9 May 1934 and was of course entered for the King's Cup race shortly afterwards. Despite achieving an average speed of 127mph, the Hornet Moth was eliminated in the heats of the 1934 race.

The Hornet Moth is also noteworthy for being one of the first aircraft to be exhaustivity tested prior to being offered for sale. Although standard practice today, it was not common for so many tests to be undertaken on aircraft. After issues with two previous designs, the DH86 Express Air Liner and the DH87 Puss Moth, de Havilland was keen to get the Hornet Moth right before it was released. The first production aircraft

left the factory in August 1935, and the aircraft type became popular in the private, club and executive markets. The Straight Corporation operated the largest single fleet of Hornet Moths, built up of ten aircraft across the south of England as part of its extensive airliner service.

One hundred and sixty-five Hornet Moths were built and around 15 survive today, most of which are still airworthy. Pictured here are two airworthy Hornet Moths: G-AHBL (pictured left) went straight into military service from the factory and was one of four Hornet Moths to be operated on floats; it is now owned by Shipping and Airlines. G-ADND (pictured below) is currently privately owned and appears here in its RAF markings, where it was registered as W9385. Finally, the aircraft pictured below is the de Havilland Museum's DH87b Hornet Moth, which was the last Hornet Moth off the production line.

Interwar light aircraft designs peaked with the Hornet Moth. The outbreak of World War Two directed all attention to the production of military aircraft. Many civil aircraft were impressed into service, and only essential civil flights could take place during the conflict. The knowledge and skills gained in the civil aviation industry during this period would prove vital to the war effort, and many young aviators could apply their civilian-learned flying skills to the defence of the country.

CHAPTER 5
THE BEGINNING OF COMMERCIAL AIR TRAVEL

Two de Havilland Dragon Rapides in formation at Old Warden Aerodrome.

The British civil airline industry was slow to start following World War One. Many European nations got a head start with financial incentives from their governments. This was not the case in Britain. The Air Ministry created the Department for Civil Aviation in February 1919, but the full scope of its responsibilities was not clear. Winston Churchill was the Secretary of State for Air at the time and he had clearly envisaged the possibilities of passenger-carrying aircraft across the British Empire, but debate continued as to whether this would be best left to private companies or to an organised governmental monopoly.

The leftover military surplus aircraft from World War One flooded the civil aviation market and prevented any new innovations in passenger transport. For now, most of the Great British public would only experience passenger flights as amusement rather than as a means of getting from A to B. Alan Cobham adapted his Avro 504 into a three-seater and began to tour England and Scotland giving joyrides. He toured extensively; his only limitation was the lack of suitable landing strips, another thing that would need addressing before passenger air travel could take to the wing in Britain.

Replica Avro 504K (G-EROE) built in Argentina and owned by Eric Alliott Verdon-Roe, grandson of Avro founder Alliott Verdon-Roe.

Entrepreneur George Holt Thomas is often referred to as the 'father of British civil air travel'. His aircraft construction company (Airco) was the largest at the time, and he was the first to form his own airline. Aircraft Transport and Travel (AT&T) was registered in 1916, three years before the Department of Civil Aviation existed. Not surprisingly, this company was the first to begin passenger and mail transport after the armistice was declared. From 25 August 1919, AT&T offered a regular scheduled service from Hounslow in England to Le Bourget in France. The company operated over 45 different aircraft types, from the DH4, which could carry two passengers, to the DH18, which could carry eight passengers.

Almost all the aircraft initially used by AT&T were ex-military and, given the infancy of aircraft design at the time, it was not surprising that the service was plagued with reliability issues. To add to its woes, Winston Churchill and the Department for Civil Aviation declared that there would be no support given and that 'civil aviation must fly by itself'. By 1921, AT&T and all its rival companies that had sprung up in the intervening years were forced to close or suspend their services. Fortunately, Holt Thomas had the foresight to form the International Air Transport Association (IATA), which laid down many regulations and procedures that provided a keystone for today's air transport industry.

The aircraft pictured here is a de Havilland DH51 known as Miss Kenya, as it was the first aircraft to fly in Kenya. The DH51 is a three-seater biplane designed and first flown by Geoffrey de Havilland in 1924. The aircraft was not a huge success, as its first engine lacked the dual ignition system required for civil use. When fitted with an improved 120hp Airdisco engine, it proved too costly to run and, subsequently, only three were ever built. Amazingly, this one has survived and remains airworthy as part of the Shuttleworth Collection. The DH51 was not used by AT&T, but it was given its markings in 2011 for filming purposes where it posed as a DH9.

Although AT&T was very much the first airline registered in Britain, it was not the only company vying for business in the aftermath of World War One. Two early rivals were the Instone Air Line and Handley Page Transport. Handley Page adapted its 0/400 bombers for transport and were up and running with regular services from Cricklewood to Paris just six days after AT&T began its first flights to France. The fares were excessive at £10 for a single ticket, but, from October, Handley Page Transport was the first company to offer an in-flight meal made up of sandwiches, fruit and chocolate. Like the other two companies, the 0/400 aircraft suffered reliability issues and, during one trip, the pilot, Captain Gordon Olley, was forced to make 17 forced landings on his way to Paris. By the time they arrived, it was too dark to find the airfield, and he was forced to land on a local football pitch.

The Instone Air Line began as a private service purely for transporting the Instone shipping company's documents and staff from Cardiff to London. It went public in February 1920 and flew an adapted Vickers Vimy aircraft, which was popular with customers. However, ultimately, like its British rivals, it could not compete with European competition, which were subsidised by their governments. The Instone Air Line ceased to operate on 28 February 1921, just over a year after its first public flight. This image shows a replica Vickers Vimy front section, which is on the wall within the events building at Brooklands Museum. It is not on show to the public, but the museum does have a complete replica onsite (see Chapter 5).

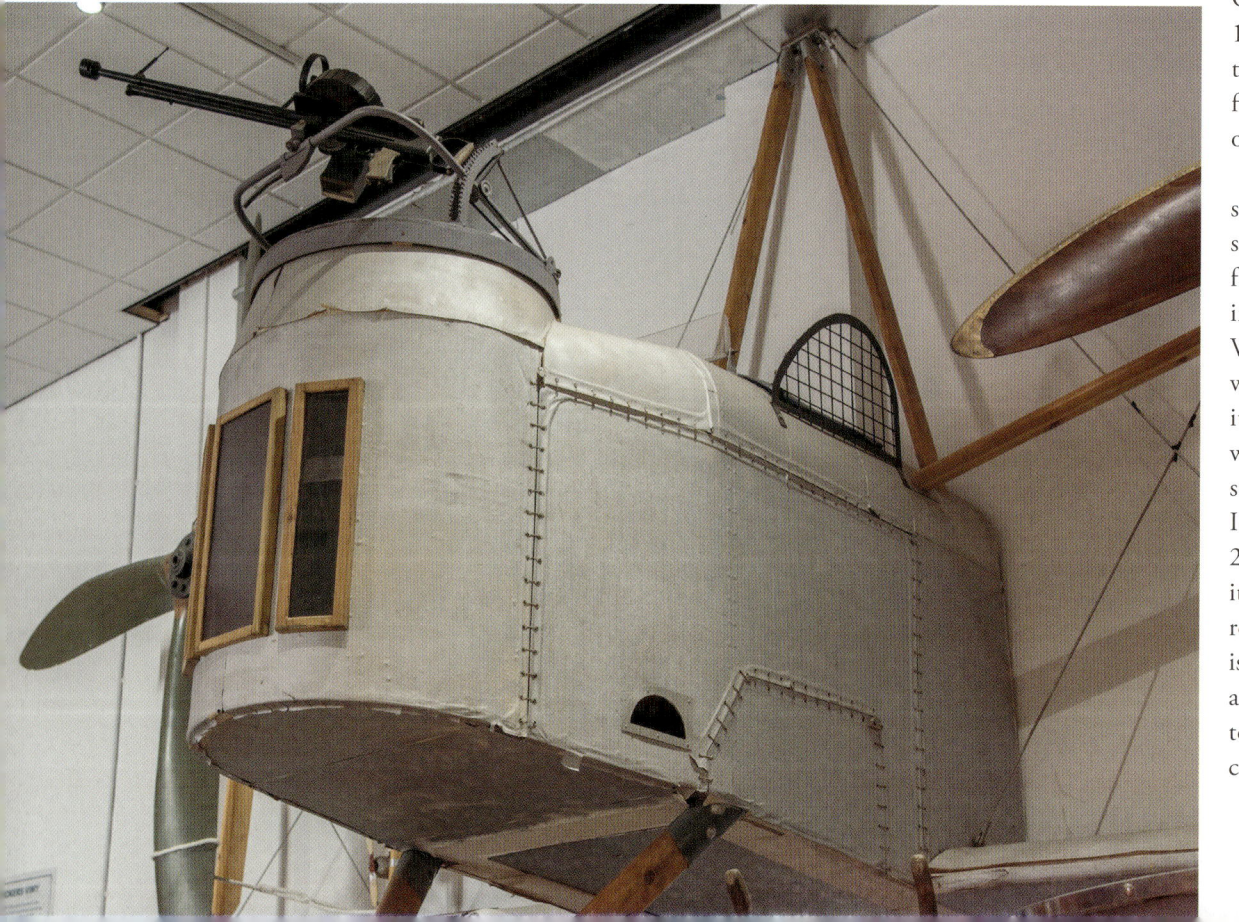

After a difficult start for British airlines, the government at last recognised that it would need to subsidise the industry if it was to keep up with European rivals. In 1923, it was recommended that the Instone Air Line and Handley Page Transport merge to form Imperial Airways. The new airline was officially created on 31 March 1924 and, crucially, was given a government grant of £137,000 in the first year. Very few aircraft types operated by Imperial Airways have survived the tests of time. The company did utilise the ex-Instone Air Line Vickers Vimy until it crashed in 1925.

Imperial Airways also operated a Desoutter Mk II aircraft as *Air Taxi Number 6* between 1933 and 1935. The Desoutter company manufactured aircraft based on the Dutch-designed Koolhoven FK41, a three-seater high-winged monoplane. It produced 41 of these aircraft in its factory at Croydon Aerodrome before the business folded in 1932. The aircraft were popular with British flying clubs but also proved successful as air taxis. The aircraft pictured here is a Mk I Desoutter built in 1931. It served as an air taxi for National Flying Services based in Middlesex for a brief period before passing into private ownership. It was eventually purchased by Richard Shuttleworth, who based the aircraft at Old Warden, where it remains to this day in airworthy condition.

Although there were other private rivals at this time, Imperial Airways dominated the market in Britain for most of the interwar years. In exchange for the government support, Imperial Airways would be limited to only using British aircraft. Whilst this was a welcome boost for the aircraft industry, it was less than ideal for the new airline, as British aircraft design lagged behind its foreign counterparts. The primary remit for Imperial Airways was to link the vast British Empire via transporting mail and personnel to the British colonies. The lack of suitable airstrips in the far-flung regions meant that flying boats were the only viable option at the time and as such made up around half of the Imperial Airways fleet, although hindsight shows that investment may have been better spent in building airstrips, as the flying boat proved to be a technological dead end.

The majority of the remaining Imperial Airways fleet was impressed into military service at the beginning of World War Two, which may account for the lack of surviving aircraft from this period. It did operate Supermarine Southamptons like the one at the RAF Museum in Hendon (pictured right), which was on loan from the RAF in 1925 until it crashed after just three months' service. Perhaps its most successful civilian flying boat was the Short S30 Empire, of which Imperial Airways operated 28 examples. The Empire was developed alongside its military counterpart, the Sunderland, in 1936. Whilst no Empires have survived, the visually similar Sunderland based at IWM Duxford is pictured here on the far right and gives some idea of how the Empire would have looked.

The Beginning of Commercial Air Travel

Around 15 other civilian airlines emerged during the 1930s, most of which were very small, operating only one or two aircraft. These companies generally concentrated on relatively short routes, and, owing to the aircraft available at the time, they could only fly small numbers of passengers at any one time. Unsurprisingly, many of these companies quickly went out of business or merged together with other smaller companies. For example, the Highland Airways, which was formed in 1933, initially flew just one aircraft, a three-passenger General Aircraft Monospar ST-4, but later upgraded to larger aircraft, such as the DH84 Dragon and DH89 Dragon Rapide. Highland Airways merged with Northern & Scottish Airways in 1937 to form Scottish Airways. Together, the companies were able to operate a larger, more sustainable fleet.

The aircraft pictured here, G-AGJG, is a de Havilland DH89a Dragon Rapide, which proudly wears the markings of Scottish Airways. The Dragon Rapide was a 1933 six- to eight-passenger biplane developed

from the larger four-engine DH86 Express Air Liner. It was produced to meet the demands for small, reliable and comfortable aircraft that could be easily operated by these smaller airlines. It was one of the most widely used interwar airliners and was also adopted by the FAA and the RAF, where it was given the name 'Dominie'. Following the war, many DH89s returned to passenger services and today over 20 examples have survived. The other aircraft pictured, G-AGSH, is wearing a post-World War Two British European Airways livery.

The de Havilland DH90 Dragonfly was the final development of the de Havilland touring biplanes. It was a tapered-wing, five-seater luxury aircraft that was visually similar to the DH89 Dragon Rapide. Structurally, it was a very different design. The fuselage was a monocoque shell built of plywood and spruce, more similar to that of the Comet Racer (see Chapter 6). The improved design gave a range of between 600 and 900 miles depending on the load and a top speed of 144mph. As was now company tradition, the prototype was entered into the King's Cup Air Race in 1936 where Geoffrey de Havilland and his son (also Geoffrey) piloted it to a respectable eighth place at an average speed of 143.75mph.

Sales of the Dragonfly were a little disappointing and relativity few were made, but two do survive today in airworthy condition, including G-AEDU pictured here. G-AEDU was built in 1937 and initially operated in Mozambique before moving to South Africa. After a long dormant period, the aircraft was restored and returned to flight in America. G-AEDU is now owned and operated by Shipping and Airlines and is based at Biggin Hill in the UK.

As aircraft technology improved throughout the 1930s, the biplane fell out of favour and the monoplane slowly began to dominate the market. Many aircraft manufacturers began to design passenger-carrying monoplanes to replace the outdated biplane designs. Sadly, World War Two would interrupt the development of the passenger-carrying aeroplane, as aircraft production soon changed focus in the build-up to war. The Avro company produced the Avro 652 airliner in 1935, which had an impressive performance for the time and, as such, was adapted to meet military specifications for a maritime reconnaissance aircraft. The resulting design became the Avro Anson (pictured at the top of this image), which would go on to serve in the RAF into the 1970s.

The Bristol Blenheim (pictured at the bottom) had similar beginnings. It was produced in response to a challenge set by Lord Rothermere, owner of the *Daily Mail* newspaper in 1934. He tasked the British aviation industry to build 'the fastest commercial aeroplane in Europe, if not the world'. The Bristol company produced the Type 142, which was designated *Britain First*. When tested, the Type 142 hit a top speed of 307mph, which, rather embarrassingly, was faster than the RAF's top frontline fighter, the Hawker Fury. It was no surprise that the Type 142 was snapped up by the Air Ministry and put into military service as the Blenheim. When World War Two broke out, the RAF had more Blenheims than any other aircraft.

The BAE System's Avro Anson teams up with the Aircraft Restoration Company's Bristol Blenheim.

Inset: **An internal shot of Avro Anson G-VROE currently based at Sleap Airfield.**

CHAPTER 6
THE GOLDEN AGE: RACING AND RECORD-BREAKING AIRCRAFT

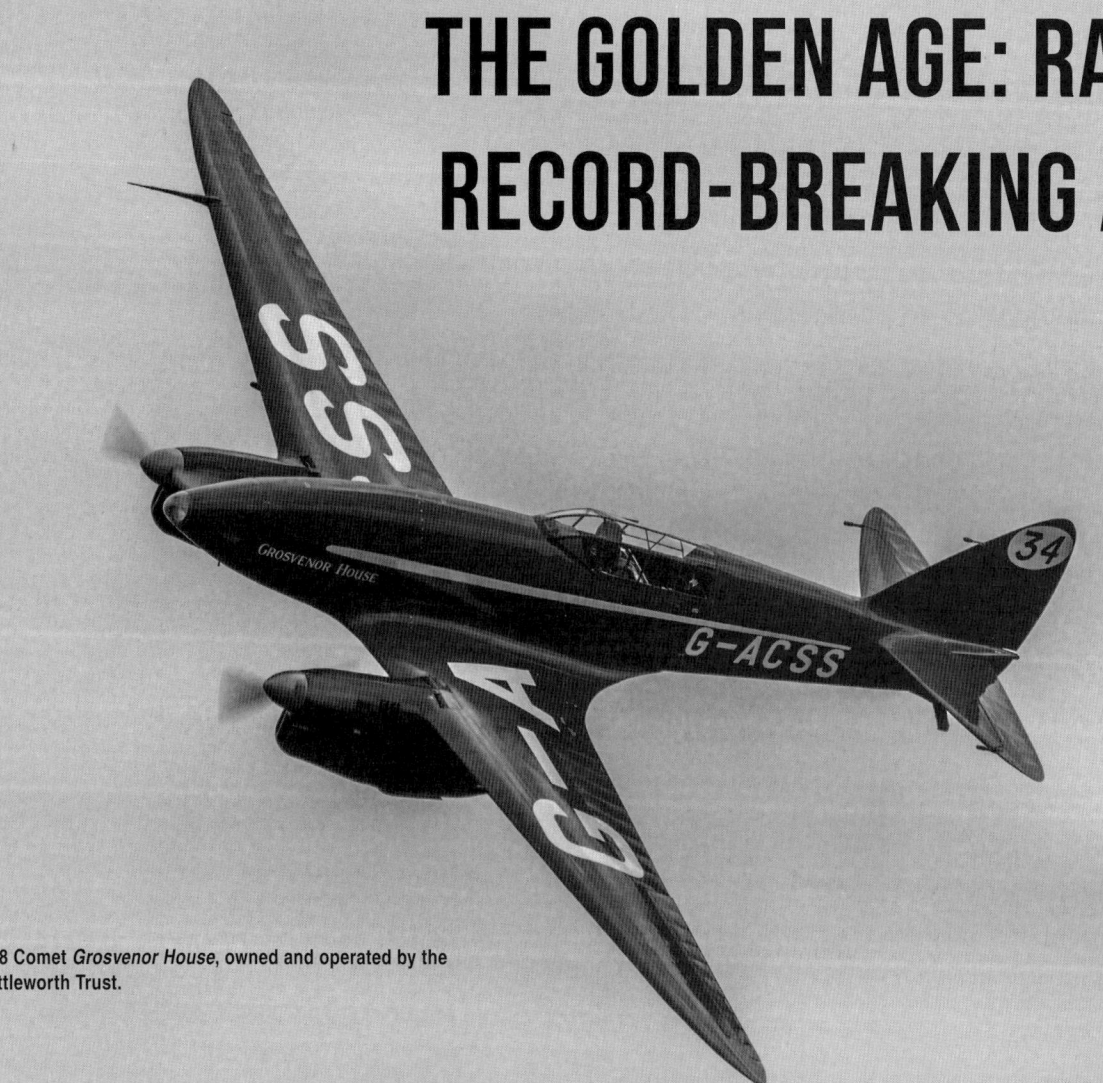

DH88 Comet *Grosvenor House*, owned and operated by the Shuttleworth Trust.

The Golden Age: Racing and Record-breaking Aircraft

The interwar period is often referred to as the Golden Age of Aviation owing to the pioneering spirit and great leaps in aircraft technology which saw records broken on a frequent basis. During peacetime, aircraft manufacturers and pilots were given the freedom to experiment and to push the boundaries and limitations of flight. Breaking records and winning races were excellent publicity for aircraft manufacturers, and it all helped to prove that powered flight was a safe and reliable means of transport. The media were desperate for aviation stories and often put up their own prizes to encourage new records to be broken. Subsequently, the pilots of the day became celebrities. The likes of Amy Johnson, the first woman to fly solo from England to Australia, and many of her contemporaries were household names.

The aircraft too became famous and, as such, there are many unique aircraft surviving today that have amazing stories to tell. The aeroplane pictured here is de Havilland DH60 Moth G-ABAG. It was built in 1929 at the Stag Lane factory and was purchased by Bentley Motors, where it was flown by many different pilots, including Amy Johnson. It passed through several private owners in its early life and competed in the King's Cup race in 1931 before being transferred to the British and Dominion Film Corporation. It is still airworthy today and is based at Old Warden Aerodrome, alongside the Shuttleworth Collection's impressive array of interwar aircraft.

At the end of World War One, the government seemed content to let British aviation fade away. Fortunately, there were a few champions keen to see the industry develop, like Lord Alfred Charles William Northcliffe, the then owner of the *Daily Mail* and *Daily Mirror*. Northcliffe was keen to create some positive news stories that his readers would relish. He targeted what many considered to be the ultimate prize in aviation at this time, the crossing of the Atlantic Ocean. Lord Northcliffe had previously put up the huge prize of £10,000 for the first non-stop flight across the Atlantic on 1 April 1913. Sadly, the advent of war prevented any real progress on this until 1919.

Eleven aircraft manufacturers expressed an interest in competing for the highly prized first Atlantic crossing, but only four companies (Sopwith, Martinsyde, Handley Page and Vickers) made it to the start line. Despite being the last to arrive, it was the Vickers team that would ultimately prove victorious. John Alcock and Arthur Brown were chosen as the pilot and navigator for the attempt in a modified Vickers Vimy. On 14 June 1919, Alcock and Brown took off from Lester's Field in Newfoundland and flew into challenging flying conditions. After an arduous journey, the pair sighted the coast of Ireland and, unaware of their competitor's whereabouts, decided to land immediately to give themselves the best possible chance of claiming the prize. From the air, the Derrygimla Bog looked the ideal landing ground, but the surface gave way on impact and the

Vimy's nose dug into the bog, leaving the tail high in the air. Alcock and Brown were unhurt, and the flight was deemed a success.

On 22 June 1919, the *Daily Mail* held a special luncheon at the Savoy Hotel, where Alcock and Brown were presented with their prize money by Winston Churchill. The feat of flying in an open cockpit through the stormy Atlantic skies with no navigational aids in an aircraft that required constant adjustment is not to be taken lightly. The flight of 1,890 miles took 15hrs and 57mins, averaging a speed of around 118mph. It would be another eight years before the feat would be repeated, when Charles Lindbergh would fly his Ryan NYP *Spirit of St. Louis* solo from New York to Paris. Despite many attempts in-between, no one could match the performance of Alcock and Brown in their Vickers Vimy.

The Vickers Vimy was designed for use in World War One as a long-range bomber capable of reaching central Germany with a one-ton payload. However, it did not begin to see service in the RAF until October 1918. By then, it was too late to see any operational action in the war. Its long-distance, pioneering flights, including the Atlantic crossing and flights from England to Cape Town and Australia, have cemented the would-be bomber's place in history. The example pictured here is a Vickers FB27 Vimy Replica (NX71MY) built in 1994 to recreate the long-distance flights of 1919 and 1920. On 3 July 2005, the aircraft achieved its primary aim when Steve Fossett and Mark Rebholz flew trans-Atlantic from Newfoundland to Ireland. NX71MY is now retired from flight but still runs up its engines at its base in the Brooklands Museum during special events.

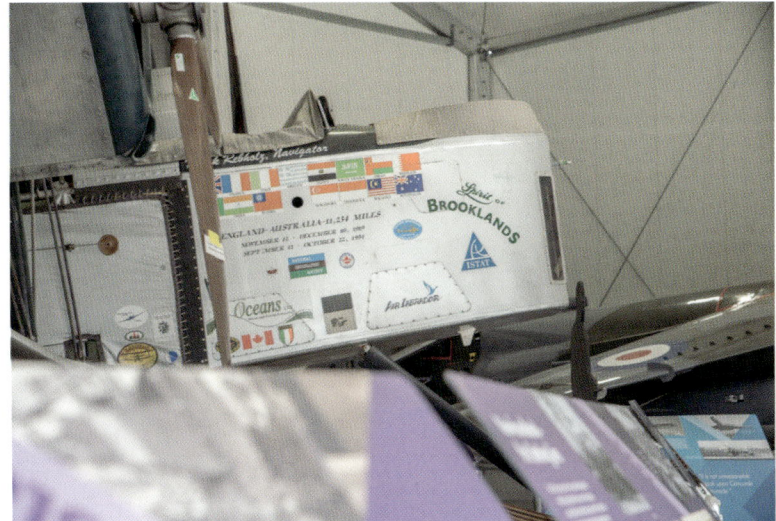

During the 1920s and 1930s, air racing was at its peak in popularity. It drew huge crowds and attracted considerable media attention. It also encouraged manufacturers to push the boundaries of what aeroplanes could do, and their daredevil pilots became celebrities and icons of the age. It became the norm for manufacturers to enter their newly designed aircraft into races, such as the King's Cup Air Race to attract publicity and sales. As aircraft designs developed, so too did the scope of air racing and it became a global sport where pilots would compete in ever more far-reaching parts of the globe.

The aeroplanes pictured here are Comper LA7 Swifts, designed by the Comper Aircraft Company in the 1930 as lightweight sporting aircraft. G-ACTF (pictured left) was initially registered in India by its owner, Alban Ali. In 1933, Ali planned to fly the aircraft to England from Calcutta but was tempted into the Viceroy's air race in Delhi en route. Ali achieved an average speed of 124mph across the 700-mile race and was awarded second place. When Ali continued his journey, he suffered engine failure over Egypt and the Swift was eventually transported to England by ship and sold to a new owner, who re-registered the aircraft as G-ACTF. Today, G-ACTF is still airworthy and is now owned and operated by the Shuttleworth Trust at Old Warden, Bedfordshire.

The Swift pictured below on the right (G-ACGL) was owned and raced by Alex Henshaw, who achieved notable success in it, including a victory in the 1933 King's Cup. Some of Alex Henshaw's other exploits are discussed later in this chapter.

The Schneider Trophy race was one of the most prestigious races during the Golden Age. Jacques Schneider founded the international competition in the early 1910s to encourage development of seaplanes. The first two races were held in Monaco in 1913 and 1914, but Schneider had to suspend the contest for World War One. When the race was able to resume, it became a matter of national pride, and government-backed military aviation teams made up the competition rather than independent civilians. The race soon became a three-way contest between Britain, Italy and the United States. In 1927, Britain achieved its first of three victories. Upon securing its third victory, it was crowned outright champion, and the final curtains were closed on the Schneider Trophy races.

Britain's all-conquering machine was the Supermarine S6B, designed by R J Mitchell. It was a seaplane that had taken aircraft design to new levels in aerodynamics, airframe construction and engine power. The S6B set a new absolute air-speed record of 407.5mph. Its Rolls-Royce engine and Supermarine airframe proved a winning combination that would eventually evolve into the iconic Spitfire. The aircraft pictured here is a Supermarine S6A, N248, which competed in the 1929 Schneider Trophy race but was disqualified when it turned inside one of the marker pylons in error. It did, however, succeed in setting a new absolute air-speed record of 357.7mph. N248 is now on display at the Solent Sky Museum in Southampton.

Another prestigious air race of the period was the MacRoberston Trophy Air Race from RAF Mildenhall in East Anglia, England to Melbourne in Australia. The race took place in October 1934 and was conceived to celebrate the Melbourne Centenary. Wealthy Australian confectionary manufacturer Sir Macpherson Robertson put up a prize of £15,000 for the winner. There were no restrictions on size of aircraft or crew, and there were prizes for the outright fastest, as well as for the best performance based on a handicap system.

The de Havilland DH88 Comet was purposely designed to compete in this event. It was one of the first aircraft to feature many of the designs now standard in modern aircraft. It boasted very thin low-drag cantilever wings and a retractable undercarriage. It also featured landing flaps, a variable-pitch propeller and an enclosed cockpit. The Comet was powered by two highly-tuned de Havilland Gipsy Six Engines, which gave it a combined output of around 460hp. The de Havilland company offered the specially designed machine for the race at a subsidised price of £5,000. It received three orders.

The Comet pictured here, G-ACSS, known at the time as *Grosvenor House*, was the overall winner of the race, completing the route in 71hrs – almost 20hrs ahead of its nearest rival. It was crewed by C W A Scott and Tom Campbell Black. After the race, the DH88 Comet was evaluated by the RAF as a potential bomber but was never actually used in service. Recent evidence has even linked this aircraft to a plot to kill Adolf Hitler via high-speed precision bombing in the late 1930s.

G-ACSS would go on to break records from England to the Cape and back and also to New Zealand. Following these amazing feats, G-ACSS was left forgotten in Gravesend until it was eventually restored to static condition for the Festival of Great Britain in 1951. Following the festival, it was handed over to the Shuttleworth Trust, who led a huge project to return the aircraft back to flying condition. Eventually, with work carried out at RAF Farnborough and at Old Warden, G-ACSS flew again in 1987. The Shuttleworth Trust still maintain this historic DH88 Comet in airworthy condition.

The Golden Age: Racing and Record-breaking Aircraft

The de Havilland Aircraft Museum is currently working on a replica DH88 Comet, which was originally constructed as a copy of G-ACSS *Grosvenor House* (original pictured on previous page) for a film. It is now being restored as another one of the Comets (G-ACSR), which also took part in the MacRobertson Air Race in 1934. G-ACSR was finished in a striking British Racing green colour, as we see here. During the race, it was flown by Owen Cathcart and Ken Waller, but it was financed by racing driver Bernard Rubin. G-ACSR finished fourth overall in the race, but returned to England first, completing the round trip in a record time of 13 and a half days.

Another event that captured the public's imagination between the wars was the King's Cup Air Race, an annual handicapped race that was started by King George V in 1922 as another incentive for the development of light aircraft and aero engines. The King's Cup race attracted a wide and varied selection of entrants, from private flyers to large aircraft manufacturers. It was standard practice at that time for organisations to enter their latest designs into the race in the hope of attracting some publicity.

F G Miles of Miles Aircraft designed the Hawk Major in 1934, which was based around the new inverted de Havilland Gipsy Major engine. The aircraft proved popular and was developed into a successful RAF trainer, as well as achieving considerable success on the racing circuit. A specialised racing version known as the Hawk Speed Six was also devised specifically for air races and was fitted with a larger six-cylinder Gipsy Major engine. Only three Hawk Speed Six aircraft were ever produced.

G-ADGP was built in 1935 by Phillips & Powis Aircraft. Luis Fontes entered it into the 1935 King's Cup Air Race and competed against his sister in her Hawk Speed Six (G-ADOD). Although the aircraft showed promise, a forced landing in the 1935 race prevented any success that year. G-ADGP remained a racing aircraft right through into the 1970s, achieving many accolades and undergoing many modifications. The Hawk Speed Six now appears in its late-1930s configuration and colour scheme and was recently acquired by the Shuttleworth Collection, where it appears alongside its impressive collection of air racing aircraft at airshows.

The Percival Aircraft Company is a name synonymous with air racing and record-breaking. The company was formed in Gravesend in 1933 by Edgar Percival, who wanted to produce his own aircraft designs. After a re-structure in 1936, the company moved to Luton Airport, where it continued production and development of its popular Gull series of aircraft. The first Percival Gull was a low-winged cabin monoplane, which was powered by a Cirrus Hermes engine. It first flew in 1932 and production ran into just under 50 aircraft.

The Gull series continued to evolve throughout the 1930s, and one such variant was the four-seater Vega Gull, which was a popular touring aircraft that also achieved success in the air racing field. Over 90 Vega Gulls were built, and they were exported all over the world. The four seats and impressive performance made them the ideal light aircraft for both touring and racing. Vega Gulls achieved some notable victories, including 1936 victories in both the King's Cup Air Race and the Schlesinger race to Johannesburg. The Vega Gull was also the chosen aircraft of Alex Henshaw and his father as they surveyed the route to the Cape in preparation for a record attempt discussed later in this chapter.

Of the 90 Percival Vega Gulls built, only this one, G-AEZJ, has survived, and it remains airworthy in the UK. Not much is known of its pre-World War Two years, but it was impressed into military service with the Luftwaffe as KE+CW.

The Percival Mew Gull is considered by many to be the ultimate development in 1930s British racing aircraft. It was a lightweight, single-seater, low-winged monoplane built primarily out of wood. It was based around the already successful Percival Gull series and was powered by a six-cylinder de Havilland Gipsy engine. The Percival Mew Gull set many records during its long career and even won the King's Cup Air Race on three occasions, in 1937, 1938 and 1955. With modifications, the Mew Gull could achieve a top speed of 265mph, and it consistently recorded the fastest times in British air races until the outbreak of World War Two curtailed its success.

This Mew Gull is a replica built by businessman David Beale as a reproduction of the 1937 King's Cup-winning Mew Gull, as it was when raced by Charles Gardner. It contains many original parts, including an authentic Gipsy Six engine, and was based around the original drawings. It first flew in 2013 and has been seen regularly at UK airshows and often appears alongside the only surviving original Mew Gull at Old Warden Aerodrome.

One of the most remarkable achievements in aviation between the two world wars was the solo record-breaking flight of Alex Henshaw to the Cape and back in 1939. In 1937, Alex Henshaw acquired Percival Mew Gull G-AEXF and immediately won the 1937 Folkestone Trophy with an average speed of 210mph. Henshaw then handed over the Mew Gull to Essex Aero, who made some dramatic modifications, including a new Gipsy Six R engine and a variable-pitch propeller taken from the DH88 Comet Racer G-ACSS. With these modifications, Henshaw cruised to victory in the 1938 King's Cup with an average speed of 236.25mph.

The Percival Mew Gull is considered by many to be the ultimate development in 1930s British racing aircraft. It was a lightweight, single-seater, low-winged monoplane built primarily out of wood. It was based around the already successful Percival Gull series and was powered by a six-cylinder de Havilland Gipsy engine. The Percival Mew Gull set many records during its long career and even won the King's Cup Air Race on three occasions, in 1937, 1938 and 1955. With modifications, the Mew Gull could achieve a top speed of 265mph, and it consistently recorded the fastest times in British air races until the outbreak of World War Two curtailed its success.

This Mew Gull is a replica built by businessman David Beale as a reproduction of the 1937 King's Cup-winning Mew Gull, as it was when raced by Charles Gardner. It contains many original parts, including an authentic Gipsy Six engine, and was based around the original drawings. It first flew in 2013 and has been seen regularly at UK airshows and often appears alongside the only surviving original Mew Gull at Old Warden Aerodrome.

One of the most remarkable achievements in aviation between the two world wars was the solo record-breaking flight of Alex Henshaw to the Cape and back in 1939. In 1937, Alex Henshaw acquired Percival Mew Gull G-AEXF and immediately won the 1937 Folkestone Trophy with an average speed of 210mph. Henshaw then handed over the Mew Gull to Essex Aero, who made some dramatic modifications, including a new Gipsy Six R engine and a variable-pitch propeller taken from the DH88 Comet Racer G-ACSS. With these modifications, Henshaw cruised to victory in the 1938 King's Cup with an average speed of 236.25mph.

After yet more modifications at Essex Aero, including some extra fuel tanks, G-AEXF was ready to attempt the out-and-home Cape record. On 5 February 1939, Henshaw set off for South Africa and returned exhausted but victorious just four days and ten hours later. The record stood for over 70 years. G-AEXF was hidden in France during the war but was overhauled afterwards in time for one more King's Cup victory in 1955. Following this, the famous aircraft was left forgotten until purchased by Desmond Penrose in 1985, who, with guidance from Alex Henshaw, returned the Mew Gull to its 1939 configuration. It now flies on a regular basis as part of the famous Shuttleworth Collection, which has been the custodian of G-AEXF since 2013.

Sadly, the tension in Europe and the eventual outbreak of World War Two just a few months after the record-breaking Cape flight put a sudden end to the pioneering Golden Age of Aviation. For the next four and a half years, aviation would be purely focused on war. Many civilian aircraft were impressed into military service, and pilots, such as Alex Henshaw, would put their skills towards helping the war effort. Henshaw would go on to become the chief test pilot for the Castle Bromwich aircraft factory and would personally test over 3,000 Spitfires and 350 Lancaster bombers at considerable personal risk.

CHAPTER 7
SILVER WINGS PART ONE: MILITARY BIPLANES OF THE 1930s

The Shuttleworth Collection's Gloster Gladiator with a tractor and Hillman Minx at Old Warden Aerodrome.

During the interwar years, military aviation went under a huge transformation. Aircraft designers produced a series of ever-improving elegant and nimble biplanes, each more impressive than the last. Theses biplanes were often coated in an aluminium-based paint that gave the fabric-covered wings and fuselage extra strength and durability. The silver finish on these aircraft gave an aesthetically pleasing look that marks the interwar period. When World War Two broke out, this romantic period was brought to a sudden end. The silver paint was replaced with camouflage, and the top wing was removed as the biplane was phased out in favour of the more aerodynamic monoplane.

The Bristol Bulldog was one of the most successful designs of the period. It was developed by Frank Barnwell of the Bristol Aeroplane Company, who had started work on what would become the Bulldog in 1924. The eventual production aircraft were powered by Bristol Jupiter VII engines. The first prototype took its first flight in 1927, and the RAF immediately placed orders, praising the Bulldog for its manoeuvrability and strength. Over 400 Bulldogs were built, and although they were never required in combat for the RAF, they were sent to the Abyssinia Crisis of 1935–36 to reinforce Middle East Command. Incidentally, the Bulldog was also the aircraft that famous Battle of Britain pilot Douglas Bader lost both of his legs in. The wing tip of his Bulldog hit the ground, causing the aircraft to cartwheel during an unauthorised aerobatics display at RAF Woodley on 14 December 1931.

This Bristol Bulldog (K2227) is a Mk IIa, which remained airworthy until 1964 when it crashed at the Farnborough Airshow. Although it was thought beyond repair, the airframe was retained by the RAF Museum, which was able to contract out a re-build in 1994. After over five years of painstaking work, it was returned to static display at the RAF Museum in Hendon, where it remains today.

The Avro 621 Tutor was a two-seater radial engine trainer. It was developed during the late 1920s as a metal replacement for the ageing wooden Avro 504. It was quickly adopted by the RAF as its main primary trainer. Over 400 were taken on charge from 1933, and over 200 remained in service when World War Two broke out. It was designed in 1929 by Roy Chadwick, who would later design the Lancaster and Vulcan. The aircraft was built using a metal-welded tube construction with a fabric covering. The early examples were fitted with Armstrong Siddeley Mongoose radial engines, but later they were upgraded to the more powerful Lynx powerplant.

This aircraft, K3215, was one of only three Tutors to survive the war and the only Tutor left today. It is owned and operated by the Shuttleworth Collection in Old Warden. K3215 saw service with the RAF College Cranwell and the Central Flying School, where it remained in service as a communications aircraft throughout World War Two. Sadly, a crankshaft failure during filming prevented the Tutor from performing its planned role in the Douglas Bader biopic, *Reach for the Sky*. Today, the aircraft is still airworthy and operates the only working Armstrong Siddeley Lynx engine anywhere in the world. It currently poses as K3241 in the colours of the Central Flying School's aerobatic team.

In 1931, Blackburn Aircraft developed a new aircraft, the B2, which was designed as a military trainer. It was based on its Bluebird IV and featured a side-by-side layout in the cockpit to enable trainer and trainee to communicate effectively. At this time, most military flight schools were used to operating tandem-layout training aircraft, and, as such, aircraft like the de Havilland Tiger Moth were adopted above the Blackburn B2. Ironically now, the side-by-side layout is the preferred choice for elementary flying training. Although the Blackburn B2 was not successful in gaining any major military contracts, 42 were built and they populated the Blackburn-owned civilian training schools at Brough Aerodrome and London Air Park.

When World War Two was declared in 1939, these civilian schools made themselves busy training pilots on behalf of the RAF. Eventually, all the civilian aircraft were merged into one flight school and became the No 4 Elementary Flying Training School. Today, only one airworthy Blackburn B-2 survives. G-AEBJ is now owned by BAE Systems as part of its heritage flight based out of Old Warden Aerodrome.

Silver Wings Part One: Military Biplanes of the 1930s

The Gloster SS 37 (Gladiator) prototype was first tested at Martlesham Heath in July 1935. It reached speeds over 250mph, which was 40mph faster than the current RAF fighter planes. However, it was made obsolete by 30 October that year when the Hawker Hurricane made its maiden flight and exceeded the Gladiator's top speed by 50mph. Despite this, the Gloster Gladiator still went into service as a stopgap whilst production was set up for the new monoplane fighters.

The Gladiator features a metal frame, powerful Bristol Mercury radial engine and, for the first time on an RAF biplane, an enclosed cockpit. There are two airworthy Gladiators surviving today: L8032 (pictured here and in the cockpit close up to the right) now wears the colours of K7895, showing how the Gloster aeroplanes would have appeared in 1937. L8032 is currently based at Old Warden, and makes up part of the world famous Shuttleworth Collection. It is a regular flyer at Shuttleworth airshows and often forms up with other aircraft of the period.

The Fighter Collection's Gladiator, N5903, (G-GLAD, pictured right) is also airworthy. It was amongst the last of the Mk II aircraft built in 1939. It briefly served with No 141 Squadron at Grangemouth, near Edinburgh, but was put into storage during the early part of World War Two. It was later used for training and ground instruction and was eventually put on display at the Fleet Air Museum in Yeovilton, before being returned to flight in 2008. It is now based at Duxford Aerodrome.

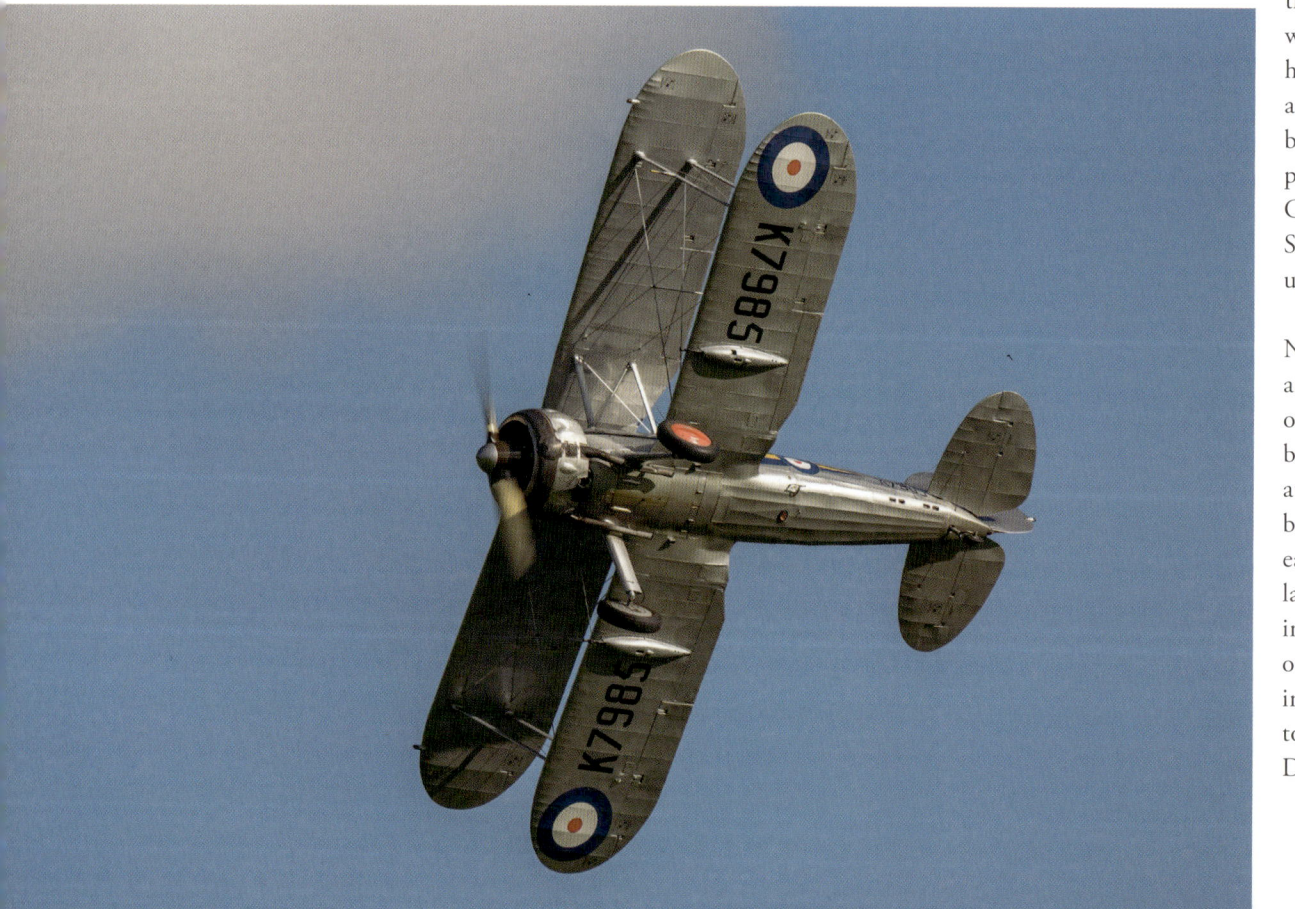

Silver Wings Part One: Military Biplanes of the 1930s

Despite their outdated design, Gladiators still fought gallantly in the early part of World War Two, undertaking several missions during the Battle of France, as well as playing a small part in the Battle of Britain. It is perhaps the No 263 Squadron Gladiators that will be remembered beyond others for their part in the war. When Germany invaded southern Norway in April 1940, 18 Gladiators were despatched on board HMS *Glorious* to provide air cover for the Allied operation on the ground. When it arrived in Norway, the advance party chose the frozen Lake Lesjaskog as the forward operating airfield. The makeshift airfield was subject to heavy bombing and, after just two days, 13 of the squadron's Gladiators were left burnt out on the ice.

Over the two days, No 263 Squadron had flown 49 sorties and engaged with 37 German aircraft, destroying six of them. Although there were no aircraft left at the end of the fighting, the squadron's personnel returned to *Glorious* to journey home. The respite was short-lived: after collecting more aircraft, they returned to Norway less than two weeks later. Tragically, *Glorious* was intercepted on its return home and sunk by the German battle cruisers *Scharnhorst* and *Gneisenau*. Almost all souls on board were lost, including the personnel of No 263 Squadron. Gloster Gladiator Mk II (N5628), pictured here, was one of the aircraft left destroyed on the frozen lake. It has been preserved in the state it was found at the RAF Museum in Hendon.

Three main variants of Gladiators were produced. The Mk II had a more powerful Mercury engine and a three-bladed metal propeller instead of the two-bladed wooden one on the Mk I. The FAA also operated a Sea Gladiator, which boosted a strengthened undercarriage, arrestor hook and a fairing for a dinghy lifeboat. Almost 750 Gloster Gladiators were built, of which more than 400 joined the RAF. Almost 100 joined the FAA, and the rest served overseas for 13 countries, including Belgium, China, Egypt and Free France.

The Gladiator's service peaked in September 1937, when the RAF had eight squadrons equipped with aircraft. By 1938, the monoplane fighters began to arrive, and the Gladiator was rapidly phased out. By the time World War Two broke out, there were very few frontline Gladiator squadrons left. Remarkably, the outdated biplane lingered on in the background and served in training and support roles for the duration of the war.

Gloster Gladiator Mk I K8042 is currently on display at the RAF Museum, Cosford. The airframe was part of the second batch of 180 Gladiators ordered by the RAF in 1935. When the aircraft eventually joined the RAF in 1937, it was sent straight to the No 1 aircraft storage unit and later transferred to No 5 Maintenance Unit (MU) in Kemble until it was sent back to Gloster to be updated.

The Gloster Gladiator represents the end of an era. As the last in a huge line of biplane fighters to serve with the RAF, it is the epitome of biplane development, with sleek aerodynamic lines, an enclosed cockpit and a Bristol Mercury engine capable of up to 700hp. Sadly, as soon as it came into service, it was already overshadowed by the new generation of monoplane fighters, such as the Supermarine Spitfire and Hawker Hurricane.

CHAPTER 8
SILVER WINGS PART TWO: THE HAWKER AIR FORCE

A rare Hawker biplane formation featuring a Hawker Demon and two Hawker Nimrods.

Although many aircraft companies were competing to produce military aircraft for the RAF during the 1920s and 1930s, there was one that dominated the market above all others. Hawker aircraft were so common during this period that the mocking nickname the 'Hawker Air Force' was given to the RAF. When the Sopwith company was forced to cease trading at the end of World War One because of excessive war profit taxes, the new Hawker Aircraft company emerged from the ashes. Although it achieved some early success, it was not until Sydney Camm became the chief designer in 1925 that the company really took off.

This image shows a trio of Hawker biplanes in formation; the Hawker Demon leads two Hawker Nimrods. The Hawker Nimrod was the naval equivalent of the Hawker Fury. Incredibly, the remains of two Nimrods were found in a scrap yard in West London during the 1970s. They were donated to the RAF Museum who eventually passed them on for restoration to flight. S1581 is now operated by the Fighter Collection; K3661 is operated by the Historic Aircraft Collection. Both remaining Nimrods are based at IWM Duxford.

In 1927, the Air Ministry was seeking a replacement for the Avro 504Ns that were starting to show their age. The Avro 504 was developed before World War One and, although it had been upgraded and proven itself as a dependable and reliable trainer, it was now very much outdated. The ministry specified that they wanted a metal-framed aircraft powered by the Armstrong Siddeley Mongoose engine. Hawker's chief designer, Sydney Camm, came up with the Hawker Tomtit. It was a single-bay biplane built from steel and duralumin tubes. For the Tomtit, the design still followed the Sopwith premise of a round, air-cooled engine up front with limited or no cowling over the engine. Whilst this made it easier to maintain in the field, it created more drag and affected the performance of the aeroplane.

Despite favourable reviews from the evaluating RAF test pilots, the Hawker Tomtit was not selected as the RAF's trainer. Instead, the Avro Tutor was chosen. Hawker still produced 38 Tomtits in total. Some were retained by the RAF for a while; others were sold to private buyers, but most wound up in aero clubs around the UK. Eventually, Supermarine test pilot Alex Henshaw acquired three of these to use as his personal aircraft, one of which (G-AFTA) survives today. It was restored by Hawker in 1949 and donated to the Shuttleworth Collection in 1960, where it is still maintained in airworthy condition today.

In 1926, the Air Ministry issued a new specification for a two-seater bomber capable of 160mph and powered by the new Rolls-Royce engine that would eventually be named the Kestrel. Sydney Camm developed the Hawker Hart in response to this ministry request. For its time, it was a ground-breaking aircraft that was 24mph faster than the required specification. With the new Rolls-Royce engine, Camm could fit an aerodynamic cowling around the front of the aircraft, which gave it its sleek look and improved performance. The Hart was also one of the first Hawker designs to feature a steel tubular frame – a technique that would be perfected and mastered by the time of the Hurricane.

Some Harts were still in service as advanced trainers at the beginning of World War Two. Famous author and fighter pilot Roald Dahl would conduct his initial training on the Hawker Hart in Iraq. Battle of Britain ace Tom Neil remarked on how he felt at home during his first flight in the Hawker Hurricane, having also trained on the internally similar Hart. There are two original Harts currently on display in the UK, one at each of the RAF Museum's sites. K4872 (pictured here) is currently on display at the RAF Museum, Cosford. It was built in 1935 and served with several flight training schools during the build-up to the war. At the beginning of 1940, it was given a brand-new Kestrel engine but remained within the maintenance unit throughout the early stages of World War Two. It returned to use as an instructional airframe in 1943.

The Hart's performance exceeded that of most of the RAF's frontline fighters at the time, prompting the request for the development of a fighter version. The Hart's outstanding design proved so successful that several other variants soon followed from the Hawker design team led by Sydney Camm: the Demon, Audax, Osprey, Nimrod, Hind, Hardy, Hartbees, Hector and Fury all share the same basic layout. The famous Hawker Hurricane is even considered by many to be the ultimate development of the Hart. Although it has lost the top wing and has a retractable undercarriage, many other design features remain in the Hurricane.

Hawker Hart II J9941 was built in 1931 as a civilian demonstration aircraft for Hawker. It was given the civilian registration of G-ABMR, and for the next five years it was used as a test bed for the ever-improving range of Rolls-Royce Kestrel engines. Later, it became the photographic chase aircraft for Hawker test flights of other new designs. When World War Two broke out, G-ABMR was given a camouflage top and yellow below paint scheme. It was then used as a company hack for ferrying test pilots. After the war, the aircraft continued its unusual and varied career. Most notably, it was entered into the King's Cup Air Race by Princess Margaret in 1951. Eventually, it found its way to the RAF Museum in Hendon, where it remains on display today.

The RAF fighter squadrons were a little embarrassed when the new Hart bombers were 10mph faster than their Bristol Bulldog fighters. As such, the Air Ministry requested a fighter version of the Hart as soon as it could be produced. Initially, this was known as the Hart Fighter, but when it arrived in RAF service it became known as the Hawker Demon. The two-seater layout was retained, but a super-charged Kestrel engine and two Vickers machine guns were fitted. Over 300 Demons were built, some remaining in service when World War Two broke out, albeit mostly as target-tugs for training purposes

Most of the 300 Demons built served with the RAF, but the Royal Australian Air Force (RAAF) also took 64 into service. Hawker Demon I K8203 (G-BTVE) is operated by Demon Displays Limited from Old Warden, Bedfordshire. It was built by Boulton Paul in 1937 and joined the RAF later that year. After a 70-year break in flying, K8203 took to the skies once more in 2009. It is seen here wearing the authentic No 64 Squadron markings that it wore in 1937. It is the only Demon in the UK, but one other is on display in Australia.

The Hawker Fury served as a frontline fighter for the RAF between 1931 and 1939. No 43 Squadron was the first to receive the Hawker Fury in May 1931, when 16 were delivered. Owing to financial cuts linked to the Great Depression, relatively few other squadrons received this new high-speed interceptor. Eventually, a few Fury Is found their way to Nos 1 and 25 Squadrons, but the slower Bristol Bulldog remained the most numerous fighter for several years. In 1936, the uprated Fury II was delivered, equipping six squadrons with the Hawker Fury in total. These remained in service until they were phased out in favour of Gloster Gladiators and Hawker Hurricanes.

The Hawker Fury pictured here (K1928) is currently being restored by the Cambridge Bomber and Fighter Society at Little Gransden Airfield. Once complete, this will go on display at Brooklands Museum. The Cambridge Bomber and Fighter Society is formed of several aviation enthusiasts. Its aim is to enhance the preservation scene in the UK by restoring aircraft. It is currently rebuilding a very early Hawker Hurricane and this Fury as a tribute to Nos 85 and 43 Squadrons, especially to their famous chief, Squadron Leader Peter Townsend. K1928 flew with No 43 Squadron, known as the 'Fighting Cocks', as it flew Gloster Gamecocks before receiving its Furys in 1931.

The Hawker Fury was the first British fighter aircraft capable of speeds higher than 200mph. The first Furys (then known as Hornets) were purchased by the Air Ministry in 1930 and subjected to several rigorous tests. It was pitted against the Fairey Firefly II, but the ministry opted for the Fury because of its all-metal construction. George Bulman took the first official Hawker Fury I on its maiden flight at Brooklands on 25 March 1931, and the first aircraft entered squadron service shortly afterwards. Around 230 Hawker Furys served with the RAF, but the Hawker Fury also served abroad for several countries including Persia, Yugoslavia, Spain, Portugal and Norway. By 1939, most Hawker Furys in RAF service had been relegated to use as trainers and ground instruction airframes. This was a wise move, as Hawker Furys remained in service with foreign air arms, such as the Yugoslav Air Force, who lost almost an entire squadron in one German attack in 1941.

The aircraft (pictured below left) is a replica Hawker Fury I (BAPC 249). It represents K5673, which was built in 1935 and delivered to No 1 Squadron in the early part of 1936. It was given the commander's 'A Flight' colours, which it wore until it was written off in a landing accident in 1938. At this time, it was patched up and transferred to No 3 Flying Training School. The replica is externally accurate, but inside it features wooden struts rather than metal as used in the original. The replica was started by the late Robin Balmer, who was a former chief designer at British Aerospace. He even worked under Sir Sydney Camm during the early phase of his career. The completed replica can be seen on display at Brooklands Museum.

Hawker Fury Mk I K5674 (G-CBZP) (pictured below right) is the only airworthy Fury in the world and is operated by the Historic Aircraft Collection from IWM Duxford. It saw service with the RAF until 1939, at which point it was transferred to the South African Air Force where it was written off after a forced landing. After almost ten years under restoration, it flew again in 2012.

The Hawker Hind was one of the last and most successful in a long line of Hawker Hart derivatives. As the clouds of war began to gather over Europe, Britain began to re-arm its military. As part of this, the Air Ministry put out Specification G.7/34 for a light two-seater bomber to replace the Hawker Hart itself. At its peak, the Hind equipped 20 RAF bomber squadrons and a further seven Auxiliary Air Force squadrons. With the Rolls-Royce Kestrel V engine, the Hind was capable of a top speed of 185mph, a range of 430 miles and a service ceiling of 26,400ft. Only one variant of the Hind was produced, although some of these were modified as trainers and for specific countries. The Hind saw widespread service across the world in countries including Afghanistan, Ireland, Latvia and Portugal.

There are at least three complete surviving Hawker Hinds left in the world today and they all come from the line that served with the Royal Afghan Air Force. The Hawker Hind pictured here (G-CBLK, L7181) was built in 1937 and issued to No 211 Squadron based at RAF Grantham for a brief period before moving to RAF Helwan in Egypt in 1938. After service in Egypt, the remaining Hinds, including L7181, were sold in April 1939 to the Royal Afghan Air Force. In 1970, the Afghan government donated four airframes to the Shuttleworth Collection, RAF Museum and National Aviation Museum of Canada, the latter receiving two airframes. At the time of writing, L7181 was stripped down at the back of the engineering workshop at Old Warden but will soon be airworthy again as part of the Shuttleworth Collection.

The Hawker Nimrod was the naval equivalent of the Hawker Fury. After the success of the Hawker Hart line of aircraft in the RAF, it was no surprise that the Royal Navy would be interested in a carrier-based version. Although the Navy usually preferred radial engines, Sydney Camm was convinced that the landplane Hawker Fury could be adapted to make a brilliant shipborne aircraft. He worked independently on a prototype and eventually the Air Ministry produced Specification 16/30 based around it. The first trial aircraft was initially known as the Norn, but eventually the name Nimrod was adopted.

A handful of Nimrods were exported for evaluation by overseas air forces, including a single aircraft each to Japan and Portugal and two to Denmark. They were intended to be built there under licence, but the advent of more advanced monoplane aircraft prevented this from happening. Before World War Two, the Royal Navy Nimrods were replaced by the Gloster Sea Gladiator. The aircraft pictured here is S1581, a Mk I Nimrod, now registered as G-BWWK. It is now owned and operated by the Fighter Collection from IWM Duxford.

The Hawker Nimrod was externally similar to the Fury. They were both single-seater biplanes with an open cockpit, fixed undercarriage and forward-firing machine guns. The first Nimrod Is entered service with the Royal Navy in 1932, equipping No 408 Flight, operating from HMS *Glorious*. Others soon followed and went to Nos 402 and 409 Flights. When the FAA was reorganised into squadrons in 1933, the Nimrods joined Nos 801, 802 and 803 Squadrons of the RAF. The Nimrod II is a very different aircraft to the Nimrod I: it has swept wings, a tail wheel, a very complex steam-condensing cooling system and a gas start system. It entered service in September 1934.

Hawker Nimrod II K3661, G-BURZ, remains airworthy and is operated from IWM Duxford by the Historic Aircraft Collection. It was one of the two aircraft discovered in a London scrap yard in the 1970s.

Most of the silver-winged Hawker aircraft that served in the British military were replaced by more modern monoplane aircraft before World War Two broke out. Very few of the types ever saw combat, which is perhaps why they are viewed so romantically today. It is only by a few twists of fate that many of these aircraft types have survived, making them extra special to see. Those remaining in service would lose their attractive silver paint schemes in favour of a more sensible camouflage paint job. Although Hawker Aircraft would continue to produce incredible aircraft well into the 1960s, its dominance as the main military provided was over.

CHAPTER 9
RE-ARMING FOR WAR: PRE-WORLD WAR TWO AIRCRAFT

A Gloster Gladiator and Hawker Hurricane in formation over Old Warden Aerodrome.

Re-arming for War: Pre-World War Two Aircraft

Political tension developed across Europe throughout the 1930s, and it soon became apparent that another war was on the horizon. The promises of peace proved to be short-lived, and whilst most nations had been following a policy of disarmament, it soon became clear that Germany was rapidly re-arming. The British government were forced to look at its home defences, and given the changes in technology since 1918, it was now likely that the next war would be a war fought in the air in a more significant way than in World War One. It was clear that Britain's air defences in the mid-1930s were not up to the task of defending the country from invasion, and so began a period of expansion that would continue well into the early parts of World War Two.

Although landplanes would dominate the headlines throughout World War Two, there was a considerable contribution from a range of huge flying boats throughout the conflict. They had a massive range and could reach areas that a land plane could not. Flying boats fulfilled many roles, including search and rescue and coastal patrols. Before the perfection of the carrier-borne fighters, they were deemed an essential part of the frontline strategy, but as technology progressed, they were phased out in this role. The Supermarine Stranraer (pictured here) was developed during the 1930s based around the Southampton flying boat. Whilst it was first rejected by the Air Ministry, the designers at Supermarine persisted with development as a private venture. Once it perfected the design, the aircraft was adopted by the RAF and served on the frontline from 1937 until 1941. The example pictured here was built in 1940 and served throughout the war for the Royal Canadian Air Force (RCAF). After the war, the Stranraer was transferred to the civil register and operated as an airliner in Canada. It is currently on display at the RAF Museum in Hendon.

Designed for army co-operation, the Westland Lysander entered RAF service in 1938. It was initially used in the opening stages of World War Two for message dropping and artillery spotting. During the Battle of France, Lysanders were also required for light-bombing duties. The *Lizzie*, as it was known, was not well-suited to such roles. Its slow speed made it vulnerable to the Luftwaffe. Later in the war, it would find its niche as a special operations aircraft. Short take-off and landing capabilities made it ideal for collecting and dropping off special agents behind enemy lines.

Westland Lysander V9312 (G-CCOM) is owned and operated by the Aircraft Restoration Company, who spent several years painstakingly restoring it to airworthy status. It is thought to be the only true 'Westland' Lysander remaining, all others remaining have several Canadian components incorporated into their re-builds. Westland Lysander V9552 was originally built for the RAF but was sent to Canada in 1942 to operate as a target-tug for the RCAF. Since 1999, it has been operated by the Shuttleworth Collection as V9367, a Mk III Lysander from No 161 Squadron. The aircraft appears in its night-time markings as used by the special duties unit from RAF Tempsford.

The Bristol Blenheim (pictured right) was initially conceived as a light bomber but was also taken on strength to Fighter Command to replace the dated Hawker Demon. Following on from its successes in World War One, the two-seater turreted fighter was considered by many to be a critical part of the RAF. Air Chief Marshal Hugh Dowding did not see the merits of such a machine, but, nevertheless, the Air Ministry felt it important to replace the ageing Hawker Demons. In 1938, the Boulton Paul Defiant (pictured below) was the obvious and preferred choice, but it would not be available in the numbers required within a satisfactory timescale. As such, the Blenheim bombers were converted to Mk I(f) fighters. It was the most numerous aircraft in RAF service by 1939, but the single-seat monoplane fighters would soon make the twin-Mercury powered Blenheim obsolete and outclassed.

G-BPIV is the only surviving Blenheim in the UK. It is a composite of a few airframes, but the aircraft takes the identity L6739 from its nose section. After a landing accident in 2003, it was decided to return the aircraft back to its Mk I configuration using a nose section that had been converted into a car just after the war. It is now maintained in airworthy condition by the Aircraft Restoration Company at Duxford. There is only one Boulton Paul Defiant anywhere in the world and it is currently on display at the RAF Museum in Cosford.

Despite the arrival of high-speed monoplanes in the mid-1930s, the biplane's day was not quite over. A few examples of biplanes were expected to hold the fort whilst production of the more modern aircraft was scaled-up. Many of these biplanes remained very much in the thick of the battle during the early stages of World War Two. The Fairey Swordfish is a prime example. It was a biplane torpedo bomber designed in the early 1930s. It was fondly known as 'Stringbag' because of its complex arrangement of struts. Incredibly, the large open cockpit biplane was still in service throughout the war, predominantly for the FAA. It found fame for its role in the sinking of the German battleship *Bismarck* in 1941 and, despite is ageing design, there were still three squadrons of them in service at the time of the Normandy invasion.

W5856 is the oldest surviving airworthy Fairey Swordfish in the world. It was built in October 1941 by Blackburn Aircraft and therefore known as a 'Blackfish'. W5856 saw service in the middle part of World War Two in the Mediterranean theatre but, by 1944, it was relegated to training duties in Canada. The aircraft took its first post-restoration flight in 2015 and currently wears the colours of No 820 Naval Air Squadron as worn during the attack of the *Bismarck* in 1941. It is one of three Swordfish operated under the Navy Wings banner. It is hoped they will all be made airworthy in time.

In the late 1930s, the RAF operated a real eclectic mix of aircraft types. There was a period of overlap as the biplane designs that had been successful for many years were replaced with more aerodynamic monoplanes. Until tested in anger, it was not always possible to predict the best layout of an aircraft for combat. The Fairey Battle was designed in the mid-1930s as a replacement for the Hawker Hind light bomber. The Battle was a three-seater monoplane powered by a Rolls-Royce Merlin engine with two .303 machine guns. It was introduced to No 63 Squadron first in 1937, but by the time war broke out in 1939, it made up 17 squadrons in the RAF.

Despite being powered by the war-winning Rolls-Royce Merlin engine that also powered the Spitfires and Hurricanes, the Fairey Battle was not fast or agile. Its defensive armament of two machine guns was also considered inadequate. The Battle did, however, achieve the distinction of being the first British aircraft to achieve an air-to-air victory during World War Two. On 20 September 1939, in a period known as the Phoney War (based on the lull of activity at the time), Fairey Battle gunner Sgt F Letchard shot down a German Messerschmitt Bf 109 during a routine patrol over the Belgium–Germany border. Despite this early success, the Fairey Battle soon showed its vulnerability and was removed from frontline service. Just a handful of Battles have survived today, including L5343, which is on display at the RAF Museum in Hendon.

The RAF had a trio of twin-engine bombers at its disposal in the late 1930s: the Vickers Wellington, Armstrong Whitworth Whitley and Handley Page Hampden. Very few complete examples of these have survived today, but there are several collections of parts dotted around the UK, some undergoing restorations, others preserved in their current state.

The Armstrong Whitworth Whitley was the first aircraft called into action during World War Two. It was tasked with dropping thousands of notelets over Germany on the very first day. The twin Merlin-engine bomber was always designed as a night-time bomber, but when the Halifax and Lancaster took over this role, the Whitely would be removed from the front line to serve as a glider tug and paratrooper training aeroplane.

The Vickers Wellington was designed by Dr Barnes Wallis (of bouncing bomb Dambusters fame). The prototype made its first flight on 15 June 1936. During the early stages of the war, the Wellington did not fare well against German fighters. Many modifications, including additional protection, self-sealing fuel tanks and redesigned hydraulics, led to an aircraft that would play a major part in bombing and reconnaissance until the four-engine heavies took over duties in the middle of the war.

The last of these bombers to enter service was the Handley Page Hampden. Around 700 of these were built, but over half were lost on operations. The Hampden was the most active of the three primary bombers during the early stages of World War Two. Seven squadrons took several missions, day and night, deep into enemy territory.

A few segments from the remains of Armstrong Whitworth Whitley R1465 at the Wartime Aircraft Recovery Group Museum at Sleap Airfield.

The recovered wreckage of Armstrong Whitworth Whitley N1498 on display at the Midlands Air Museum.

The 'Loch Ness' Vickers Wellington Mk Ia N2980 at Brooklands Museum.

Internal shots from inside a composite Vickers Wellington fuselage at Brooklands Museum.

Vickers Wellington T.10 MF628 currently undergoing restoration at the RAF Museum, Cosford.

Handley Page I P1344 undergoing restoration at the RAF Museum, Cosford, soon to be on display at Hendon.

The Hawker Hurricane is famous for its role in the early part of World War Two. It shot down more enemy aircraft than any other Allied fighter in the Battle of Britain. It was introduced to the RAF in the late 1930s and, by the time the war broke out, it was the most numerous Allied single-seater fighter. Its history can be traced back to the Hawker biplane fighters discussed in the previous chapter. By the mid-1930s, Sydney Camm felt that he had maximised the potential that a biplane could offer. An advancement in technology meant that losing the top wing, which was hitherto essential for structural support, was now a reality and the potential of the monoplane could be unlocked.

Sydney Camm took his idea of a new monoplane fighter to the Air Ministry. It was initially unconvinced. Nevertheless, with the backing of the Hawker board, Camm set to work on his new monoplane fighter. By 1934, heads began to turn at the ministry. The new design boasted an extra 80mph on its predecessors. This was partly due to its new PV 12 Rolls-Royce engine that would soon evolve into the world-beating Merlin. The prototype first flew in 1935 and became the first fighter anywhere in the world capable of over 300mph. Although revised slightly, the Mk I Hurricane was the main operational Hurricane until the Mk IIs appeared in June 1940. There are presently six Mk I Hurricanes on display in the UK, including four airworthy examples. There are also two static examples of this early variant on display in the Science Museum and the RAF Museum in London.

Hawker Hurricane Mk I P3717 (G-HITT), a recovered wreck from Russia, restored by Hawker Restorations, is now based at Old Warden.

Hawker Hurricane Mk I V7497 (G-HRLI), restored by Hawker Restorations, is now based at Duxford.

Above left: Hawker Hurricane Mk I R4118 (G-HUPW), recovered from India by Peter Vacher, is now owned by Hurricane Heritage and based at Duxford.

Above right: Hawker Hurricane Mk I P2902 (G-ROBT), a recovered wreck that crashed near Dunkirk, is now based at Duxford. The black and white underside was designed to enable ground observers to gauge distance and direction but was phased out after a few months in favour of a more discreet sky camouflage.

Right: Hawker Hurricane Mk I P2617 on display in No 607 Squadron markings at the RAF Museum, Hendon.

On 3 June 1936, the Air Ministry contracted Hawker to build 600 Hurricanes. The first production Hurricane Mk I made its first flight on 12 October 1937, then fitted with a more powerful Merlin II engine. By the end of 1937, Hurricanes were being delivered to the RAF. The first of these had fabric-covered wings, which were reported to blow out during high-speed flights. The first Hurricane pilots also experienced their machine guns freezing at altitude. By 1939, all new Hurricanes were built with stressed-skin metal wings, and heating units were fitted to the wings to overcome the teething troubles.

There are over 70 Hurricanes surviving across the world today in various states of preservation, from crash remains to fully restored flyers. In the UK, there are ten that are currently airworthy, although thanks to the hard work of aircraft restorers such as Hawker Restorations the number is increasing. Hurricane Mk I L1639 initially served with No 85 Squadron in the Battle of France. It is now being restored to static running condition by the Cambridge Bomber and Fighter Society at Little Gransden Airfield in Cambridgeshire. Eventually, it will go on display at Brooklands Museum.

The Spitfire was developed by R J Mitchell and the team at Supermarine, using their success with a series of racing seaplanes as a starting point. The first flight took place in 1936, just four months after the Hurricane, but delays in early production meant that it was not available in the same numbers when World War Two broke out. Very early Mk I Spitfires were built with a two-bladed fixed-pitch propeller, which was quickly upgraded to a three-blade de Havilland two-pitch version for later production models. Like the Hurricane, the early Spitfires experienced issues with the Merlin II engine and were also uprated to the Merlin III early on. The early Spitfires were capable of up to 367mph and had a range of around 300 miles. The Mk Ia was armed with eight 0.303in Browning machine guns. Experiments took place with canon-armed Spitfires during the early phases of the war, but they were not operational until much later.

Seven complete Mk I/Mk Ia Spitfires can currently be seen in the UK. Three of these are airworthy; the others are in museums. The RAF Museum has two, one at each location, whilst the IWM and the Science Museum both keep one each on display in London. K9942 is the oldest surviving Spitfire anywhere in the world. It took its first flight on 21 April 1939 and was allocated to No 72 Squadron before the outbreak of war. K9942 saw extensive action over northern France at the start of Operation *Dynamo* but landed wheels up on 5 June 1940, which, in effect, saw an end to its operational career. Most of the early surviving Spitfires are Mk Ias, but K9942 is a rare Mk I, initially fitted with a Merlin II engine.

The early Spitfires were a far cry from the final marks that ended World War Two. They were limited in range, so only 15mins of actual combat time could be expected with the engines at full power. They also lacked canons, which the German fighters had much sooner than the RAF interceptors. The Spitfire's closest rival, the Bf 109, had a Daimler-Benz 601 engine, which had fuel injection that enabled inverted flight. The carburettor-fed Spitfire, however, would experience fuel starvation and the engine would cut out if this was attempted. Despite these early limitations, the Spitfire was agile and, in many ways, a superb fighter from the start. The main issue in the build-up to war would be production; far fewer Spitfires had arrived at the frontline than expected by the time the war broke out.

Squadron Leader Geoffrey Stephenson flew Supermarine Spitfire Mk Ia N3200 on its one and only mission on 10 May 1940, shooting down a Ju 87 before being forced to make a crash landing on Calais beach.

There are four Mk I Spitfires that remain airworthy in the world today. One of these is now based in America but, for a short period of time, all were together in the UK at the IWM, Duxford. The Biggin Hill Heritage Hangar are also working on a few Mk I restorations, including P9372, a Battle of Britain veteran.

The Supermarine Spitfire was the ultimate development in pre-World War Two aircraft. It was the fastest, most agile interceptor that the RAF had going into war. It was developed and proved itself time and time again as the war progressed but was not available in great numbers until the middle of 1940. A fighter aircraft capable of well over 300mph was inconceivable at the end of World War One, but aviation had clearly made some huge leaps forward during the interwar years.

Supermarine Spitfire Mk Ia X4650 is currently operated by Comanche Warbirds and is based at Duxford in the UK. It currently wears its authentic No 54 Squadron markings, as worn in 1940.

Above: Supermarine Spitfire Mk Ia P9374 is now based in the US, but it was restored by the Aircraft Restoration Company at Duxford.

Below: Supermarine Spitfire Mk Ia X4590 on display at the RAF Museum, Hendon.

Above: Supermarine Spitfire Mk Ia AR213 is currently painted to represent a No 71 Eagle Squadron machine, P7308. After suffering a landing accident in November, AR213 was struck off charge but would eventually be made airworthy again to appear in the *Battle of Britain* movie.

Below: Supermarine Spitfire Mk Ia P9372 is in the early stages of restoration at Biggin Hill Heritage Hangar.

CHAPTER 10
SUMMARY

A Gloster Gladiator biplane peels off from the formation, leaving the skies to the Supermarine Spitfire monoplanes.

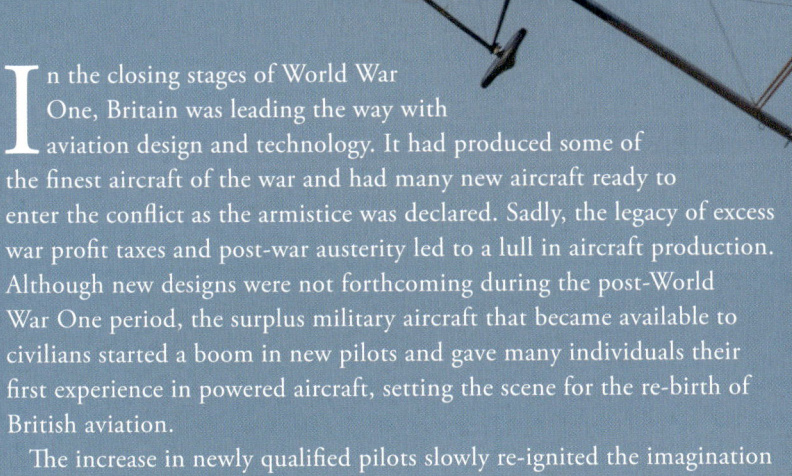

In the closing stages of World War One, Britain was leading the way with aviation design and technology. It had produced some of the finest aircraft of the war and had many new aircraft ready to enter the conflict as the armistice was declared. Sadly, the legacy of excess war profit taxes and post-war austerity led to a lull in aircraft production. Although new designs were not forthcoming during the post-World War One period, the surplus military aircraft that became available to civilians started a boom in new pilots and gave many individuals their first experience in powered aircraft, setting the scene for the re-birth of British aviation.

The increase in newly qualified pilots slowly re-ignited the imagination of aircraft designers and their newest designs were built purely for civil aviation. Aircraft became ever more comfortable for touring and more efficient and cost effective for the private pilot to operate. Suddenly, aviation became more accessible. It was not until the 1930s that the focus of aircraft design turned once again to military purposes.

A Sopwith Camel and a Royal Aircraft Factory SE5a.

With no wars to fight, aircraft designers were able to concentrate on pioneering, racing and record-breaking, leading to a boom in the popularity of air racing and increased public interest in pioneering pilots. Initially, adapted World War One military aircraft were used for long-distance flights and races, but as time progressed, purpose-built racers were conceived. The performance of many of these racing aircraft was often better than the frontline military aircraft of the time. It was the racing industry that encouraged the developments in technology that ultimately lead to the high-speed fighters.

Today, the sight and sound of 1930s racers in the skies provokes romantic feelings of the Golden Age of Aviation, when powered flight had an innocence about it; aircraft were not built for war or profit, just for the joy of flying or for the thrill of the chase.

DH88 Comet racer leading two Percival Mew Gulls.